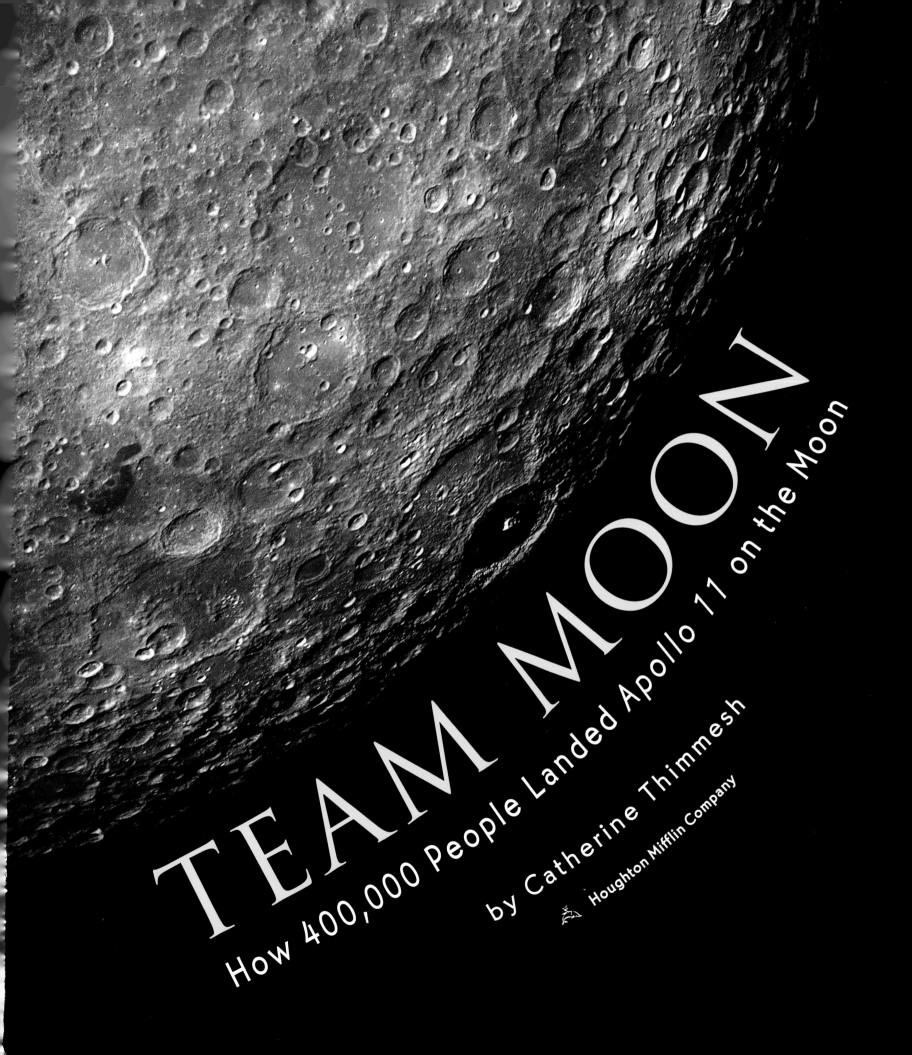

TEAM MOON

How 400,000 People Landed Apollo 11 on the Moon

by Catherine Thimmesh

Houghton Mifflin Company

For the kids of all those thousands and thousands of people who worked on Apollo. For the sacrifices you made—the birthday parties, ballgames, and bedtime stories that your parents had to miss because the moon was calling, and demanding their time. It must have been hard sometimes. But look at what they did! Thanks for sharing them with the world when we needed them most.

And for TeamMoon—all four hundred thousand of you—scattered around the United States, the globe; some, sadly, passed on. At age two and a half, I missed the main event. But hardly an evening goes by that I don't find myself momentarily transfixed by that glowing sphere in the sky. I'm arrested and awestruck at first by its sheer beauty; and then, by an awareness—trying to suppress both smile and tears—"My God, they actually did it!" All I can say is thank you.

To the memory of Max Faget, NASA chief engineer and space guru, who would not allow his ailing health to disrupt his generosity of spirit and agreed to speak with me during my research to share his enormous knowledge of Apollo in hopes of inspiring the kids of today.

www.houghtonmifflinbooks.com

The text of this book is set in Martin Gothic.

Library of Congress Cataloging-in-Publication Data

Thimmesh, Catherine.
Team Moon / by Catherine Thimmesh.
p. cm.

ISBN 0-618-50757-4 (hardcover)

1. Project Apollo (U.S.)—Juvenile literature. 2. Apollo 11 (Spacecraft)—Juvenile literature.
3. Space flight to the moon—Juvenile literature. I. Title: Team Moon. II. Title.

TL789.8.U6A582546 2006
629.45'4—dc22
2005010755

ISBN-13: 978-0618-50757-3

Printed in Singapore
TWP 10 9 8 7 6 5 4

THE FLIGHT PATH OF *APOLLO 11*
TO THE MOON AND HOME AGAIN

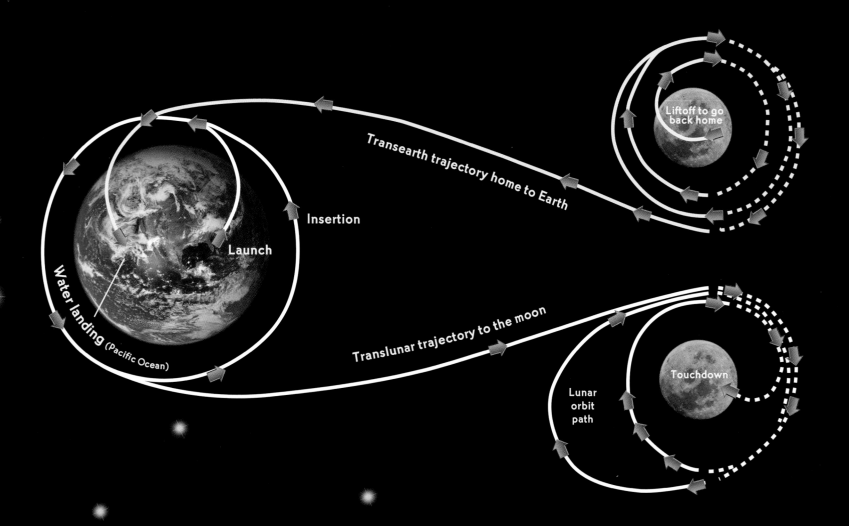

Insertion

Launch

Water landing (Pacific Ocean)

Transearth trajectory home to Earth

Liftoff to go back home

Translunar trajectory to the moon

Lunar orbit path

Touchdown

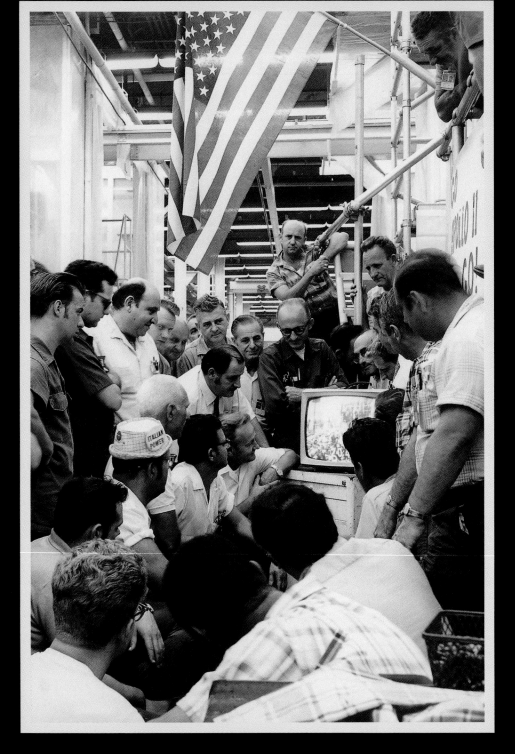

Beyond Imagination

It was mind-boggling. The television itself had been a flat-out miracle when it began to dominate the scene a mere twenty years previous. And now, that techno-logical wonder of wonders was going to trump itself. Because very soon, if all went according to plan, it would transmit pic-tures of an actual man, on the actual moon. In 1969, on July 20 (in one part of the world) and July 21 (in the other part), half a billion people on the blue-marbled globe clicked on their TV sets—flush with anticipation—eager to watch as *Apollo 11* would attempt to put man on the moon for the first time in all of history. The *moon!*

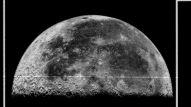

(p.4) A crowd of workers from Grumman—the company that built the lunar module—squeeze together in Plant 3 at Bethpage, New York, to witness the launch of *Apollo 11*. (photo courtesy Grumman History Center) (p.5) Despite rain, thousands of New Yorkers attend a "moon-in" at Central Park's Sheep Meadow, watching the live moon telecast projected on a big screen, enthusiastically waiting for Neil Armstrong to set foot on the moon. (photo courtesy of Corbis)

And now, at this defining moment, the world had come together—like nothing ever before—not only to wish the astronauts Godspeed, but to bear personal witness to this incredible event. On that day, people gathered: in homes and schools and businesses; in restaurants and shops; and on sidewalks and streets and in parks. They were eager to be a part, however small, of something so out-of-this-world big. If there was a TV in the vicinity, it was on. And people sat. And watched—wide-eyed, waiting.

"Fate has ordained that the men who went to the moon to explore in peace will stay on the moon to rest in peace. . . . These brave men, Neil Armstrong and [Buzz] Aldrin, know that there is no hope for their recovery. But they also know there is hope for mankind in their sacrifice."

Rest in peace? On the moon? Thankfully, no; those ominous words (penned in top secret for President Nixon) were never spoken. But while millions upon millions of people were spellbound and starry-eyed with moon mania (sitting, watching, waiting), those people behind the scenes fretted over more problems and concerns and plans for emergencies than the rest of the world could ever know. The "Fate Has Ordained" speech was to be delivered in the event that the worst possible scenario came to pass. The speech's very existence proved that, beneath all the excitement, those people running the show never for a moment lost sight of the all too real dangers they were choosing to run into head-on. And though millions of eyes were focused front and center on the astronauts and the spacecraft, much of the action would, in fact, be taking place on the sidelines.

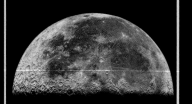

(p.6) A small television at an outdoor sidewalk café in Milan, Italy, draws a large crowd of spectators for the momentous landing. It didn't matter that Neil and Buzz were Americans. They were mankind's representatives, they were "men from the planet Earth." [So said the plaque they would leave on the moon.] (photo courtesy AP/Wide World Photos) (p.7) In the Firing Room, members of the launch team view the liftoff after *Apollo 11* has cleared the tower and is on its way to the moon.

When those millions of people tuned in hoping to witness the moonwalk, one thing they wouldn't see (or at best might just catch a glimpse of) were the nonastronauts, those beyond the glare of the limelight. The regular folks whose efforts made an impossible mission possible in the first place. All the people behind the scenes whose ideas and expertise, imagination and inventiveness, dedication and focus, labor and skill, combined in one great endeavor—on the grandest of grand scales—and conspired to put man on the moon. Yes, three heroic men went to the moon; but it was a team of *four hundred thousand* people that put them there. They were the flight directors, controllers, planners, and engineers; the rocket designers and builders and technicians; the managers, supervisors, quality control and safety inspectors; the programmers, electricians, welders, seamstresses, gluers, painters, doctors, geologists, scientists, trainers, and navigators . . .

Apollo 11 is their story too.

Astronauts Neil Armstrong, Michael Collins, and Buzz Aldrin in the hatchway of the command module during a testing session.

"All this is possible only through the blood, sweat, and tears of a number of people. . . . All you see [are] the three of us, but beneath the surface are thousands and thousands of others."

—Apollo 11 astronaut Michael Collins

"I think one of the things we had was a common goal; and we all realized that we were into something that was one of the few things in history that was going to stand out over the years. We're going to go to the moon! We're putting a man on the moon!

"And that so captured our imagination, and our emotion, that we didn't want to go home at night. We just wanted to keep going, and we couldn't wait to get up and get back at work in the morning—because we're going to the moon!"

—Charlie Mars, NASA chief lunar module project engineer at Kennedy Space Center

In the Beginning . . .

They were going to the moon, all right—at least that was the plan. That was the dream and the challenge set forth by one man, President John F. Kennedy, when he declared in May of 1961:

"I believe this nation should commit itself to achieving the goal, before this decade is out, of landing a man on the Moon and returning him safely to Earth."

So they came by the thousands—kids really, twenty-somethings, a few in their thirties. No one knew for sure how to get to the moon, how to land, or get home. But their goal was clear-cut, and that was enough. That gave them purpose: a reason to puzzle out the problems and seek solutions rather than sleep.

Kennedy's decision was triggered by an intense "space race" with the old Soviet Union. The Soviets were first in space (with *Sputnik*); first too with a man in space. But for those who actually worked on the moon shot, the "race" became an afterthought. They were fueled instead by a desire to explore the heavens—the poetry of it all, the scientific challenge of it all, the *"We're going to the moon!"* excitement of it all.

But the moon? Could it really be done? Right from the get-go, administrators had identified ten thousand individual tasks that would have to be completed. And that was only the beginning. So much to do. Too much? An aide to Kennedy quietly predicted that it would take forty-four attempts. *Forty-four* tries before ever landing once on the great gray rock in the sky.

The final picture was altogether different from the dream. Most thought they'd be going straight to the moon with one spacecraft, land, and come straight back. Instead, as the plan evolved, it called for two very different craft: a command and service module for flight and a lunar module (LM) to land on the surface. No one ever imagined landing on the moon in a seatless, gold-foil-encased, four-legged, spidery-ish thingamajig nicknamed the "LEM." After all, no one knew what a lunar module was even *supposed* to look like. And so, form followed function. Never mind if it looked like a bug.

"I can't say that I'm aware of any program where more people understood what the schedule was, how important it was, and worked so hard to make it happen. We had a great team," recalled Joe Gavin, vice president of the Grumman Aerospace Corporation, contractor for the lunar module.

That team at Grumman was 7,500 workers strong. They designed, developed, and built the lunar module, christened *Eagle* for *Apollo 11*, from the ground up. Reliability was insisted upon. They had a motto: *There is no such thing as a random failure.* And failures were eliminated—one by one. Because it was *their* baby, *their* handiwork—eight years of *their* lives—that, very soon, would settle down (fingers crossed) on that giant glowing ball in the inky-black soup of space.

(p.11) The lunar module, or LM (pronounced "lem"). She was LM 5, but the crew named her *Eagle*. The LM was mainly designed and built by NASA's prime contractor, the Grumman Aerospace Corporation. The LM is about 23 feet high and 31 feet across the extended landing-gear pads. Its total Earth weight, fully loaded with crew and propellants (fuel), is 32,200 pounds.

And Onward . . .

Space . . . it's dangerous out there: micrometeoroids, radiation, airlessness. And coming home would be no picnic either. The compact-car-size space capsule would be greeted and surrounded by searing white-hot flames as it slammed madly back down to Earth.

"In designing the command module, the one thing we had to be sure of was that we could keep the crew alive— that was a big item," said Max Faget, NASA chief engineer and principal designer of the command module.

Keeping the crew alive under such extreme conditions was indeed a big item. Only the command module, *Columbia*, would make the complete journey from Earth to the moon and back home again. It would serve as crew living quarters and as the spacecraft control center. And *Columbia* alone would confront the fiery Earth reentry.

But the wizards at North American Rockwell (NASA's prime contractor for the command module) were up to the

challenge. Fourteen thousand folks there, plus a skilled hodgepodge of eight thousand other companies, toiled to ensure that millions of components on the command module were in top-notch order.

Columbia was off to confront danger. Its builders would need to rely on their eight years of effort to give them confidence for a successful outcome. But it would be five hundred thousand miles before the truth of the matter would be told. Could their command module keep the crew alive?

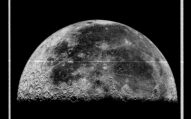

(p.12) Command module 107, along with the service module, or CSM, was built primarily by North American. Named *Columbia* by the crew, the command module was crafted with more than 2 million parts; nearly 15 miles of wire; a control panel with 24 instruments, 566 switches, 40 indicators, and 71 lights. (p.13) *Apollo 11* during the CDDT, the dress rehearsal for launch. "*[You] look out at the dark-blue, before-dawn morning and it is absolutely magnificent. . . . Majestic.*"—Ernie Reyes, chief of the Pre-flight Operations Branch.

And Upward . . .

Launch operations at Kennedy Space Center (KSC) in Florida was like its own little town. A whopping seventeen thousand engineers, technicians, mechanics, contractors, and managers were needed to pull together the Apollo 11 launch. Needed to check, check, check the spacecraft: test it, stack the three rocket stages in the vehicle assembly building, or VAB, roll it out, recheck it, fuel it, and ready it for liftoff.

One of the most critical preparations for launch was the orchestration and performance of the crucial CDDT.

"The Countdown Demonstration Test, or CDDT, gives us confidence that we're going to get there in time and everything's going to percolate [work perfectly] together," explained Ernie Reyes, chief of the Pre-flight Operations Branch for Apollo 11. *"It's a dress rehearsal for the countdown. The only thing we don't do, is we don't load the vehicle with all its fluids and juices [rocket fuel]."*

Come launch day, Ernie Reyes and about five hundred others would work the consoles from the Firing Room of the Launch Control Center (LCC), the nucleus of launch operations. They would run the controls that would catapult *Apollo 11* moonward bound. Five thousand others would directly support them for the actual liftoff.

It was a long, long march to that day, and the little town of KSC became a second home to quite a few folks. Many a lunch—dinners, anniversaries, birthdays—were forsaken in pursuit of Ready to Launch. On July 16, 1969, they were indeed ready. And at 9:32 A.M. . . . *whoosh!*

(p.14) Launch of *Apollo 11* as viewed from an air force plane. *Apollo 11* rockets to the moon on the *Saturn V* launch vehicle. Made up of three stages, the *Saturn V* is an intimidating 281 feet. (p.15) A view of Earth from orbit. The rocket has put *Apollo 11* into a circular orbit 115 nautical miles above Earth. The crew will remain in this "parking orbit" for 1 1/2 orbits (revolutions around Earth) while they check out the spacecraft systems. Midway through the second orbit, the third stage of the *Saturn V* will ignite to send them on a translunar trajectory (pathway to the moon). When they arrive at the moon, they will go into lunar orbit—circling and studying the moon (and eating and sleeping) for 12 revolutions. On the 13th orbit, the *Eagle* will undock from *Columbia* and prepare for descent.

Maiden Voyage . . . The Final 10 Miles

"*The* Eagle *has wings!*" radioed Neil Armstrong from the lunar module as he and Buzz Aldrin flew sixty-nine miles above the moon. Four words. Slightly cryptic, but oh so lyrical. There was no doubt of their meaning: The lunar module *Eagle* had separated from the command module *Columbia* and was now flying solo. It was ready to descend to the surface of the moon. Magical words, those four. Big smiles back on Earth, back in Houston, at Mission Control.

In Houston, the White Team was at the consoles in the control room monitoring and facilitating the moon landing. Gene Kranz was the flight director on duty—the person in charge of the mission during that time and responsible for the final decisions. He had arrived at the Mission Control complex (MCC) shortly past dawn, accepting the good lucks that were tossed his way by those he passed in the lobby. He refused the elevator, instead climbed three flights of stairs to the MOCR (Mission Operations Control Room, pronounced *MOE-ker*). They were attempting to put man on the moon today—a dazzling technological triumph—but at home, technology had a habit of getting stuck between floors, and Flight Director Kranz was taking no chances. "*Today is not the day to get stuck in an elevator,*" he wrote in his memoir.

Forty minutes prior to beginning the landing sequences, Kranz addressed his flight controllers:

"In the next hour we will do something that has never been done before. We worked long hours and had some tough times but we have mastered our work. Now we are going to make this work pay off. You are a hell of a good team. One that I feel privileged to lead. Whatever happens, I will stand behind every call that you will make."

It was time. As instructed by Mission Control in Houston, astronauts Neil Armstrong and Buzz Aldrin fired their descent rocket engine, lowering the *Eagle* to an altitude of just 50,000 feet above the moon's surface. (On an earlier mission, several months previous, *Apollo 10* had gotten to this very point—50,000 feet—close, but still so far.) But now, for the first time, Neil and Buzz would go that last leg—the final ten miles.

"You are Go for PDI [powered descent ignition]," Mission Control radioed the crew.

Never had more monumental words been spoken so simply: The green light was given to go ahead and land on the moon. Twelve minutes, now. And they would be on the surface of the moon. Or not.

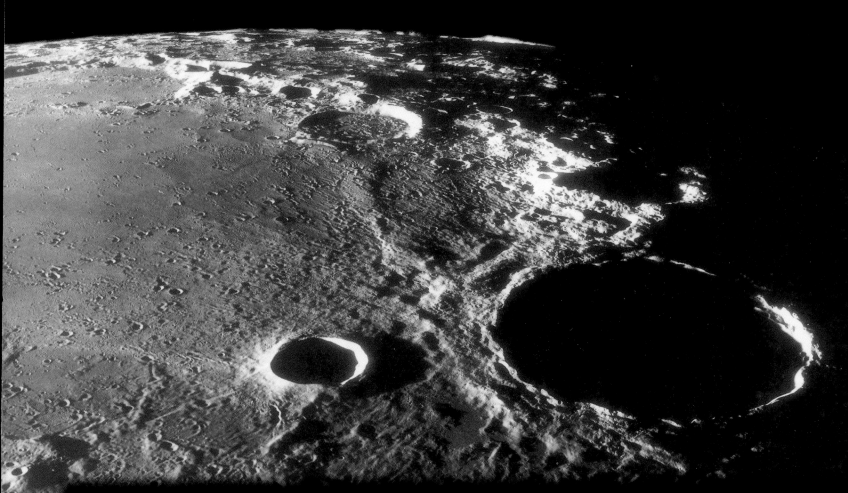

(p.16) The *Eagle*, shortly after undocking from *Columbia*. Mike Collins is doing a visual inspection of the LM from *Columbia*, paying particular notice to the landing gear (that it is in the down and locked position). (p.17) *Apollo 11* captured this view of the large crater Theophilus (about 60 statute miles in diameter), along with the smaller crater Madler (14 statute miles), at the northwest edge of the Sea of Nectar on the lunar near side.

Challenge 1: Alarms

BAM! Suddenly, the master alarm in the lunar module rang out for attention with all the racket of a fire bell going off in a broom closet. *"Program alarm,"* astronaut Neil Armstrong called out from the LM ("LEM") in a clipped but calm voice. *"It's a 'twelve-oh-two.'"*

"1202," repeated astronaut Buzz Aldrin. They were 33,500 feet from the moon.

Translation: *We have a problem! What is it? Do we land? Do we abort? Are we in danger? Are we blowing up? Tell us what to do. Hurry!*

In Mission Control, the words TWELVE OH TWO tumbled out of the communications loop. The weight of the problem landed with a thud in the lap of twenty-six-year-old Steve Bales. Bales, call name GUIDO, was the mission controller for guidance and navigation.

A moment earlier (after some worries with navigation problems), Bales had relaxed with a deep breath, thinking at last: *We're going to make it.* Now, wham! His mind, again sent racing; his blood rushing; his heart fluttering; his breath—still as stone. But he wasn't alone.

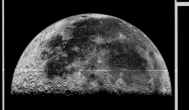

(p.18) A view from lunar orbit from the LM window near the beginning of the descent. Captured as a still image from the 16mm film camera mounted in the LM, this shows the LM's descent (about 33,000 feet.). (p.19) This series shows the LM pitching over (from its back) and the lunar horizon coming into the crew's view.

A voice on another loop—belonging to one of Bales's backroom support guys, twenty-four-year-old computer whiz kid Jack Garman—burst in to make sure Bales was aware of the 1202. A quick glance at a master list told them a 1202 was *executive overflow*. Simply put, the computer had too much to do. But program alarms, as Garman knew firsthand, were built into the computer solely *to test the software*. By their very definition, they weren't alarms that should happen in flight. (During development, these alarms were testing computing cycles.)

Yet there it was: 1202. An unreal reality. First, stunned inactivity at Steve Bales's console.

Then, a bombardment of thoughts: *What's the problem? Do they land? Do they abort? Are they in danger? Are they blowing up? Tell them what to do. Hurry!*

Bales scoured his guidance and navigation data.

Searching. Sifting. Sorting.

Flight Director Kranz plucked details from a flood of incoming information.

Juggling. Judging.

Backroom guy Jack Garman (call name AGC) consulted his handwritten program alarm list, mandated by Gene Kranz (and neatly stashed beneath the Plexiglas on his console).

CapCom Charlie Duke (or Capsule Communicator, the voice link between Mission Control and the spacecraft) mused aloud: "*It's the same one we had [in the simulator].*"

And indeed, in one of the very last simulations, or practice sessions, before liftoff of *Apollo 11*, mission controllers found themselves stumped when faced with a similar program alarm. While training with the backup crew, SimSup Jay Honeycutt (or Simulation Supervisor) had asked software expert Jack Garman to concoct some sort of computer glitch for the controllers to solve. So Garman remembered the hidden software testing alarms and threw out one of those. It wasn't a 1202, but a similar type—one that supposedly *should never happen in actual flight* (because the situations that would trigger those alarms had presumably already been removed from the software).

During that simulation, that test, GUIDO Steve Bales had called for an abort—an immediate end to the landing. They stopped the pretend-land on the moon. But it was the wrong call. While the computer was definitely having difficulties, it would still have been safe to continue the landing because the LM's critical functions were still working.

"And so [Flight Director] Gene Kranz, who's the real hero of that situation, sat us all down and said, 'You WILL document every single program alarm, every single possible one that can happen' and what we should do about it if it happens," recalled AGC Jack Garman, explaining how they ended up with a written record of those "nonexistent" program alarms.

Sometimes, after the bugs have all been removed during development, programmers might go back in and remove all their testing alarms. But often, it's considerably more efficient (and cheaper) to just leave them buried unseen, deep down in the software.

(p.20) The *Eagle* on approach to the moon. (p.21) The moon, as it looked from the lunar module, closer to landing.

"So I remember," continued Jack Garman, *"going back to my little corner with my friends—my col-leagues—and we wrote them all down. Wrote them on a sheet of paper (twenty or thirty of these alarms that were not supposed to happen), taped this list to a piece of cardboard, and stuck it under-neath the Plexiglas on the console."*

As they would discover later, though it seemed an impossible situation, it wasn't a false alarm. Executive overflow meant the computer was too busy. And the computer was too busy (it turned out) because a switch had been mistakenly left on.

"Give us a reading on the 1202 program alarm," said Armstrong from the lunar module as it contin-ued its rapid—and very real—descent to the moon.

"The astronauts had no idea what these alarms were," explained Garman. *"Absolutely no idea. These alarms were software development alarms. They'd never seen them. Never studied them. Never had them. No one in Mission Control knew what they were, not Kranz or anybody."*

GUIDO Steve Bales determined the computer had not lost track of the LM's altitude or speed—critical for avoiding a lunar crash—and still had its guidance control, also essential. Flight Director Gene Kranz determined, with input from his controllers, that all other systems were functioning within acceptable parameters. AGC Jack Garman concluded that as long as the alarm didn't recur, they were okay.

Garman prompted GUIDO Steve Bales, who gave the "Go" to Flight Director Kranz, who in turn gave the command to CapCom Charlie Duke. CapCom relayed the message to Armstrong and Aldrin. *"We are Go on that alarm,"* he told Neil and Buzz and the hundreds of others listening in on the loops. Not more than twenty seconds had passed from the time the 1202 was first called out.

"Program alarm!" Buzz responded from the LM. "Same one."

Garman clarified to Bales that as long as the alarm was not constant—not continuous—they were okay. The rest of Bales's information looked good. He told the Flight Director, *"We're Go."* Flight Director Kranz "went around the horn"—polling his controllers for their status reports—they were all "Go." Kranz told his voice link to the astronauts, *"CapCom, we are Go for landing."*

Aldrin acknowledged the good-to-Go. They were 3,000 feet from the moon now.

"Program alarm!" Buzz called. "1201."

"When it occurred again a few minutes later," Jack Garman recalled, *"a different alarm but it was the same type . . . I remember distinctly yelling—by this time yelling, you know, in the loop here—'SAME TYPE!' [in other words, Hang tight!] and he [GUIDO Steve Bales] yells 'SAME TYPE!' I could hear my voice echoing. Then the CapCom says, 'SAME TYPE!' Boom, boom, boom, going up."*

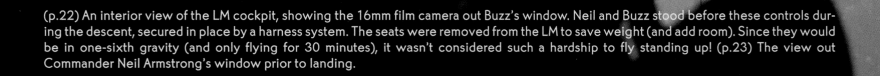

(p.22) An interior view of the LM cockpit, showing the 16mm film camera out Buzz's window. Neil and Buzz stood before these controls during the descent, secured in place by a harness system. The seats were removed from the LM to save weight (and add room). Since they would be in one-sixth gravity (and only flying for 30 minutes), it wasn't considered such a hardship to fly standing up! (p.23) The view out Commander Neil Armstrong's window prior to landing.

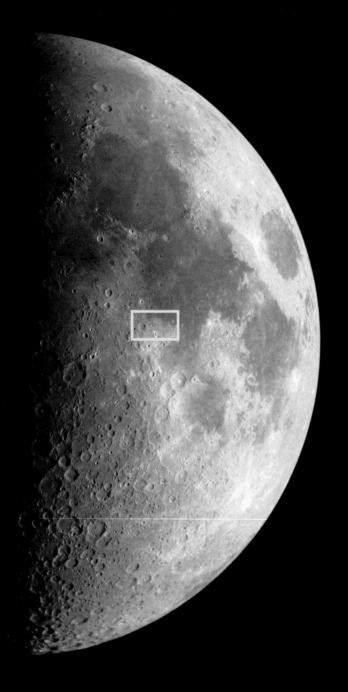

Their voices were rapid-fire. Crisp. Assured. There was no hesitation. But you could practically hear the adrenaline rushing in their vocal tones, practically hear the thumping of their hearts as the alarms continued to pop up.

Then the *Eagle* was down to 2,000 feet. Another alarm! 1202. Mission Control snapped, *Roger, no sweat.* And again, a 1202! Then the *Eagle* was down to 700 feet, then 500. Now, they were hovering—helicopter-like—presumably scouting a landing spot.

In hundreds of practice simulations, they would have landed by now. But Mission Control couldn't see the perilous crater and boulder field confronting Neil and Buzz. Those things, coupled with the distraction of the alarms, had slowed them down.

More than eleven minutes had passed since they started down to the moon. There was only twelve minutes' worth of fuel in the descent stage.

(p.24) Telescopic views showing the area of the *Apollo 11* landing site: *Tranquility Base.* The half-moon images were photographed from a home balcony in Dassel, Germany. (courtesy photographer Ulrich Lotzmann) (p.25) Telescopic half-moon image. (courtesy photographer Ulrich Lotzmann)

Challenge 2: Almost Empty

"Sixty seconds!"

Not sixty-one. No wiggle room. No "just a couple more seconds—we're almost there." And no second chances. They had just sixty seconds to land on the moon.

Absolutely no one expected it to happen. They painstakingly planned so it absolutely wouldn't-couldn't happen. But here they were, less than five hundred feet from the moon, and just about plumb out of fuel.

Robert Carlton, the CONTROL position in Mission Control, who was in charge of monitoring fuel consumption among other things, had just sent the shocking sixty-second notice through the voice chain up to the astronauts. Both Neil and Buzz knew when they heard the words "sixty seconds," that was how much time remained until they *had* to abort. Until they *had* to push the button, fling themselves away from the moon, never to land. Or else, they could possibly die.

we wanted to give him [Neil] every chance to land," explained Robert Carlton. "So we wanted it [the LM] to be as near empty as it could possibly get, but on the other hand, we didn't want him to run out of gas ten feet from the surface. That would have been a bad thing to do, you know. So you had to hit both. You wanted to make the mission, but you didn't want to jeopardize your crew, and you wanted to play it just as tight as you could safely."*

The heavier the spacecraft, the harder it is to launch. And fuel is heavy. So it was critical to pinpoint the fuel needed, add a cushion, then take no more than necessary. But now, because the landing was taking far longer than planned, the fuel was almost gone. Mission Control wanted Neil to take as much time as he needed and fly the LM as near empty as possible *only* because they wanted him to make the landing. But if he ran out of fuel above the surface, in all likelihood the LM would crash onto the moon. So they were trying to time it to the last possible second before calling an abort—calling off the landing.

If they aborted, if they flung themselves away from the moon (never to land), they would be slung into lunar orbit, where they would meet up with Mike Collins in the command module and head home to Earth. If they landed, though, leaving the moon wouldn't be a problem because there was a full tank of fuel in the ascent stage for liftoff (an abort also used the ascent stage). But the ascent and descent stages were completely separate. When the supply for the descent stage was empty, that was it. Sharing fuel was not an option.

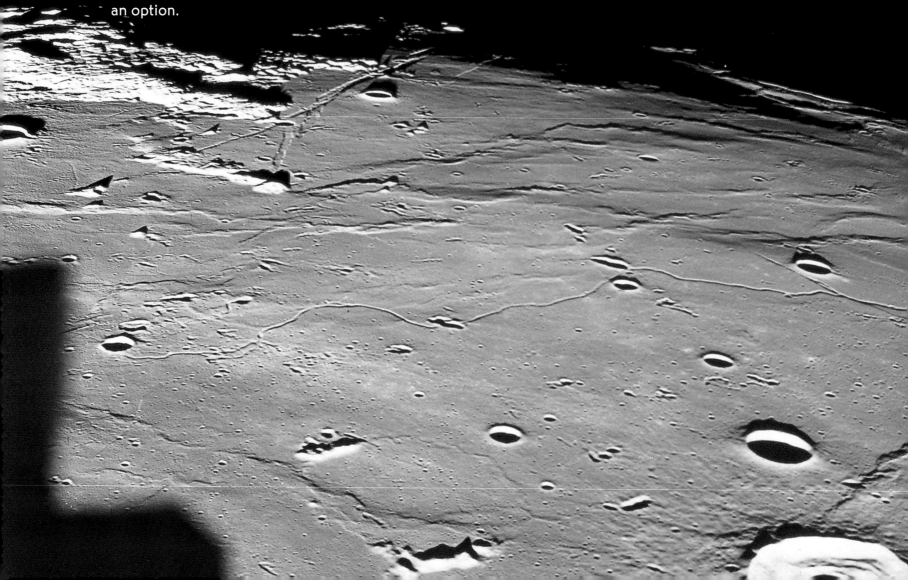

In every simulation, the LM had been landed well before the low-level sensor was tripped, indicating 120 seconds of fuel left. Bob Nance, backroom support for CONTROL, was calculating the seconds of fuel remaining on his paper strip chart. (Flight Director Gene Kranz would write in his memoir, *"I never dreamed we would still be flying this close to empty and depending on Nance's eyeballs."*) Bob Carlton backed up the backup with a stopwatch.

Thirty seconds!

Now would not be the time for the two Bobs to miscalculate, miscount, or lose their superhuman powers of concentration. They could not afford to be wrong.

"When we tripped low level, things really got quiet in that control center," recalled Bob Carlton. *"We were nervous, sweating. Came to sixty seconds, came to thirty seconds, and my eyes were just glued on the stopwatch. I didn't see [the control center as a whole]. The system could have [fallen] apart at that instant, and I wouldn't have [known] it. I was just watching the stopwatch."*

Eighteen seconds!

Click.

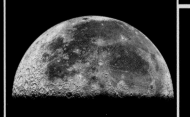

(p.26) A view from orbit of the *Apollo 11* landing site in the southwestern Sea of Tranquility. The landing area is located in the smooth area at the top to the right just before the shadow. (p.27) A view of the lunar surface shortly after landing, with the thruster visible in the foreground as seen through Neil's window.

People [were] concerned about the amount of fuel you had left, the master alarms. . . . I don't believe anybody in the room breathed for the last five minutes. We were just hanging on every word. And trying to force the vehicle down by sheer willpower. Get down! Get down! *Neil, get down. Turn off that engine.*"
 —*Charlie Mars, chief lunar module project engineer; listening in on a headset in one of the backrooms at the Mission Control complex*

"Forty feet, down two and a half, picking up some dust . . . "
—Apollo 11 astronaut *Buzz Aldrin, from the LM*

"You know it's real when you walk in [to the Mission Control building]. Then you sit down and start doing what you've done a hundred times and it becomes surreal—you don't know or care if it's real, you're just doing your thing. And then all of a sudden it doesn't go quite the same. Somebody calls out something that brings you . . . wakes you up—and says 'Oh my God it is real!' And that was what happened when he said 'We've got some dust.' We'd never heard that before."

—AGC Jack Garman, in Mission Control

"Houston, Tranquility Base here. The Eagle has landed."
—Apollo 11 commander Neil Armstrong, from the LM

"Roger, Tranquility. We copy you on the ground. You got a bunch of guys about to turn blue. We're breathing again. Thanks a lot." ("I was so excited," Duke later said, "I couldn't get out Tranquility Base. It came out sort of like Twangquility.")
—CapCom (and astronaut) Charlie Duke, in Mission Control

Challenge 3: Frozen Slug

After eight challenging years and countless hours, man was finally on the moon. Flight Director Gene Kranz would soon "go around the horn" for the very first Stay/No Stay decision.

"You know, they landed, and everybody's cheering and everything and then all of a sudden somebody notices that something's gone wrong. Temperature's building up. Uh-oh! It shouldn't be like that," explained Grumman engineering manager John Coursen.

Up, up, up went the temperature in a fuel line on the descent engine. Up, up went the pressure. Rocket science rule number one? Do *not* allow the fuel to become unstable. Instability equals unpredictability—and unpredictability is just another word for random explosions and all sorts of unwanted chaos.

Engineers John Coursen, Manning Dandridge, and a whole lot of others sprang into action. Back at the Grumman plant in Bethpage, New York (where Coursen was stationed), there was a frenetic burst of engineering pandemonium:

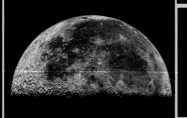

(p.30) A view out the LM window just after landing. The astronauts could tell just from looking that the surface was very fine-grained and that there was a surprising number of rocks of all sizes. (p.31) Just after landing, the LM's shadow is cast on the moon, with the horizon of the moon visible in the distance.

from table to table, rushing;

blueprints and schematics, unfurling;

telephones, dialing;

telephones, ringing . . .

Do you remember that one test? What about when such and such happened? Remember when so-and-so talked about . . . Any ideas? . . .

At 300 degrees, the fuel was quickly approaching its 400-degree instability rating. Engineers at Grumman, and their counterparts at NASA in Houston (like Grumman manager Tom Kelly), simultaneously deduced the likely culprit: a slug. A solid slug of frozen fuel had trapped a small amount of the descent fuel in the line. This caused the temperature and pressure in the line to rise rapidly—and dangerously.

"First thing we did was get the drawings out so you could see," recalled John Coursen. "All kinds of functional diagrams, say of the heat exchanger; the line that runs from there to the valve of the tank. . . . You want to get all of the data before you that you can; and that's the purpose for having a good call room back at the plant—because there's more data there that the people didn't take with them [to Houston]."

Up went the pressure, the temperature—now 350 degrees. Terrified of an impending explosion (even a small blast could damage vital engines or components), Coursen and the Grumman engineers argued their options. They could (1) abort now and leave the problem on the moon. (The slug was isolated in the descent stage—and liftoff relied on the separate ascent stage. The descent stage—no longer necessary—would be left behind.) Or they could (2) try to "burp" the engine—give the valve a quick open-close to release the built-up pressure.

The trouble with option 2 was that the venting might push the fuel to an unstable condition. Or, another possible outcome of the "burping": what if the landing gear hadn't deployed correctly? Could any move-ment, or any resulting burst—no matter how small—tip the LM over? Many a voice in the debate thought the safest option was to abort—now! But that opinion was quickly overruled by the Grumman and NASA leadership (who were confident of the landing gear), and the consensus of the leaders was that it would be safe to gently, *gently* burp the engine.

Suddenly, though, just as the procedure was about to be relayed to the astronauts, the pressure . . . the temperature . . . dropped! And . . . stayed down. The frozen slug, apparently, had melted! (Probably due to the extreme heat in the fuel line.) Problem solved. And only now—a solid, panic-stricken, gut-wrench-ing, heart-palpitating ten minutes by clock but feeling like an eternity later—did it sink in for John Coursen, Tom Kelly, and a lot of the other Grumman folks who had poured years of their lives into build-ing the lunar module: Their baby was on the moon. Let the cheering begin!

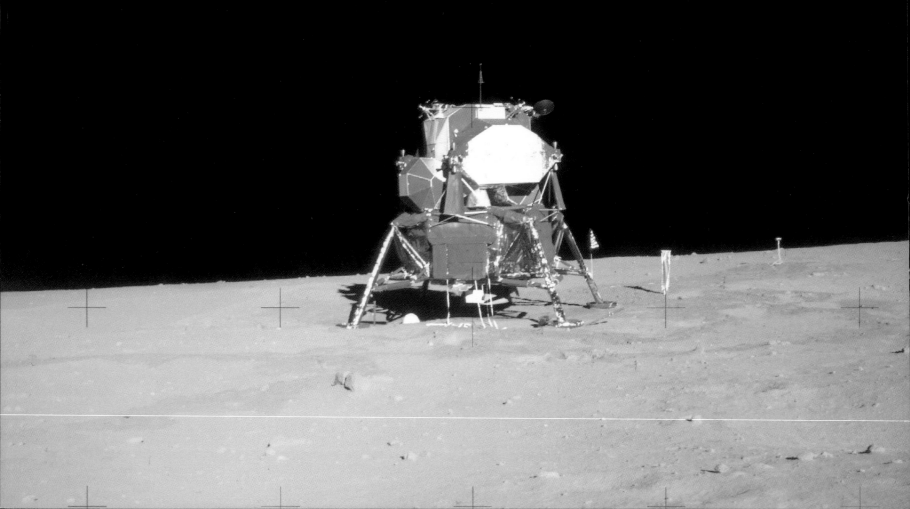

"I'm going to step off the LM now."
—Neil Armstrong, from the moon

"That's one small step for man, one giant leap for mankind."
—Neil Armstrong, first man on the moon

Challenge 4: First Steps

"The design goal of the space suit was to give man enough mobility to get out and walk—and the key word there is walk—*on the surface of the moon," explained Richard Ellis, an employee of ILC Dover, the company NASA contracted with to build the space suits.*

But between the micrometeoroids (specks of rock in space), the lack of oxygen, the searing 250-degree heat in the sun, and the bone-chilling minus 250 in the shadows, walking on the moon would clearly be no walk in the park.

It would take roughly five hundred people working over several years between NASA and ILC Dover (plus their many subcontractors) to create the Apollo space suits. Suits that would protect the astronauts from the lethal hazards of a space environment, as well as enable them to take a stroll on the moon's surface.

"Reaching down is fairly easy."
—*Buzz Aldrin, from the moon*

"The space suit in itself is probably a little more than half engineering and the rest art," said NASA Apollo space suit subsystems manager James McBarron. *"And by art, I mean there was a series of trial-and-error attempts that led to the successful design."*

Some of that trial and error was provided by Richard Ellis of ILC Dover, whose medium, astronaut-like body size qualified him for the job of space suit test subject. Whether he was walking on a treadmill, climbing in and out of a capsule mock-up, or maneuvering around the LM, his ability to move was the key. But that mobility was drastically hindered by pressurization—adding oxygen to the closed environment of the space suit—without which the astronaut would instantly die.

So, the engineers tested joints—knees, ankles, elbows, shoulders, hips—different materials, different positionings. They tested fabrics. And fabric combinations. Restraint cables. Airtight seals. Comfort. Durability. And the mechanics of this, the technicalities of that. And the slightest of movements.

(p.34) Buzz Aldrin collects core samples (soil beneath the surface) from the moon. He attempts to drive the core tube into the surface by hitting it with a hammer. The astronauts were surprised at the resistance they met in the compacted soil: Buzz was unable to get the core tube in farther than a few inches. (p.35) Buzz deploys the EASEP's passive seismic experiments package. The goal of the experiment was to measure meteoroid impacts and moonquakes to help determine the inner structure of the moon.

I would just put the suit on," recalled Ellis, "become pressurized, and stand in front of a grid back-drop. And they would photograph; and I would go through a series of predetermined motions so they could say, 'Well, he's reached three degrees further with this configuration, but can't reach downward as well.' A lot of analyzing and engineering evaluations went on."

"Traction seems quite good."—Buzz Aldrin

"People don't realize one of the few pieces of equipment that . . . had to work from launch to return back from the moon was the suit," said NASA's James McBarron. "Very few pieces of equipment actually flew the whole mission. . . . [The suit] had to interface with the command module couch and launch support system, the command module navigation and optics. Then it had to interface with the LM environmental control system and instrumentation system for landing, its navigation system and all its displays. Then it had to be able to work with the portable life support system, and then all the way back. That's quite an integration job."

And so complex was that integration job that each and every design change had to be made within the strict constraints of the many interface requirements. In other words, special rules applied. If a segment of the suit interfaced with another system (connected up and became compatible with it), that portion of the suit couldn't be altered by any design changes in any way. Alterations had to be made around it.

"It's absolutely no trouble to walk around."—Neil Armstrong

Each astronaut on the *Apollo 11* prime crew had three suits custom-made for him: two that were flight-ready and one for training purposes only. Twenty-two layers—including Nomex, neoprene-coated nylon, Beta cloth, Kapton, and Mylar—were stitched, glued, and cemented together to create the total suit assemblage. This was done by a team of specially trained seamstresses at ILC Dover. There was a comfort liner, a nylon bladder to retain pressure, convolutes (coils) for movement, and layers for thermal and micrometeoroid protection.

"We made up each layer separately for the whole suit: the arms, the legs, the body," recalled seamstress Eleanor Foracker of ILC Dover. "Some of them were taped together, some of them were sewn together. And then we plied them up: one layer on top of another layer. . . . And then we would make the cover layer and the liner so that we could fit this ply-up inside—and that's how the suits were put together."

The lunar boots were actually a slip-on overshoe. Design was tough. No one knew for sure what to expect on the moon's surface. Would they encounter deep dust and get trapped? Sharp rocks that would slice open a hole in the boot?

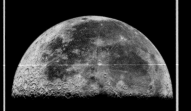

(p.36) The astronauts deploy the U.S. flag on the moon. The image was captured by the 16mm camera mounted on the LM. There is a metal rod on the top of the flag to hold the flag out. Without it, since there is no wind on the moon, the flag would just droop down. (p.37) Buzz said he needed to be careful to keep track of where his center of mass was while moving on the moon. It took a couple of steps for him to make sure his feet were underneath him. He concluded that the best method of moonwalking was the conventional one foot after the other. This image was captured by the 16mm camera attached to the LM.

"I approved the design of the lunar boots," recalled NASA's James McBarron. *"I was just hoping that what we planned for . . . well, that there were no surprises; like we'd end up with deep dust that the boot wouldn't handle, or a surface characteristic that would cut the boots."*

And of course the boots, like the suits themselves, went through seemingly endless rounds of testing. Since walking was the primary goal, an ankle convolute was necessary to allow for ankle extension and flexion—the natural movements made by the foot when walking.

"I spent a lot of time walking on a treadmill. And they tried out lots of combinations of convolutes and various pulleys with ropes and cables—while they photographed just the action of my ankles and feet," remembered Richard Ellis, ILC Dover test subject.

Quality control—a critical component of the entire Apollo program—was of the utmost importance. Inspectors checked each individual suit piece before it was assembled. Then they inspected the assembly before it was plied up. Finally, the full suit was inspected from head to toe. The thermal micrometeoroid outer covering was even x-rayed. The teeniest, tiniest details were documented. On paper.

James McBarron explained how it would be possible for him to trace the metal from, say, the aluminum neck ring on the suit to the ore it was fashioned from, to the actual mine from which that ore was originally pulled. Such linkage made problem solving quicker and easier.

"When it came time you had a problem that needed to be worked," McBarron said, *"you could relate one piece of equipment to another, back to its source lot, where it was manufactured or processed."*

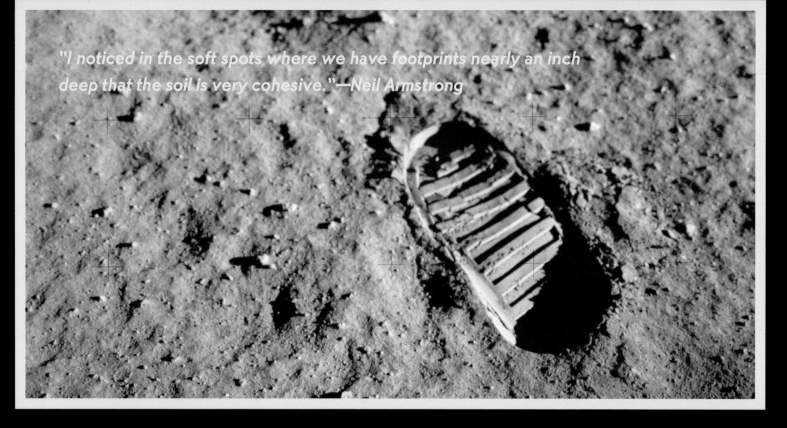

"I noticed in the soft spots where we have footprints nearly an inch deep that the soil is very cohesive."—Neil Armstrong

When *Apollo 11* launched for the moon, Richard, Eleanor, and James—along with their colleagues at ILC Dover and NASA—were confident about the suits. Still, there were the unknowns. And that caused some anxiety.

Seamstress Eleanor Foracker remembered a comment made by the ILC Dover president that reflected how many of the suit makers felt: *"Like our president said,"* Eleanor explained, *"'We didn't worry too much until the guys on the moon started jumping up and down. And that gave us a little bit of an eyebrow twitch, because if they had burst the inner bladder to their pressure suits, they would have lost pressure. That was our worst fear.' But I didn't feel that was going to happen because those suits had been tested so much."*

And those suits had been tested so well. They were a triumphant success, of which there is evidence aplenty—thanks to an environment free from wind and atmosphere. For captured on the surface of the moon—for near eternity—are man's footprints, crisp and clear, pressed purposefully and magnificently into the lunar dust.

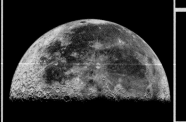

(p.39) A TV camera was placed on the moon. The camera would transmit pictures at a different rate from those on standard televisions. An electronic system developed by the RCA company converted the "slow scan" TV signals to commercial standards so they could be broadcast over the airwaves.

Challenge 5: Wind

Whistling and howling, a fierce wind whipped through the Australian grassy paddock—probably scaring the bejeebers out of the grazing sheep. It slammed smack into the Dish, causing its gears to screech and groan. Simultaneously, a shrill alarm pierced the inner air of the Dish (officially known as the Parkes Radio Telescope), warning those inside of the perilous winds now in full force outside. And, not unlike the 1202 master alarms that had shaken Neil and Buzz a few hours earlier (in the LM), this alarm blast startled the daylights out of those gathered in the telescope's main control room. But despite the noise, the crew inside would need to concentrate.

Because people cared—a great deal—about the *visual*. And it was the *visual* the guys at the Dish were responsible for. Right about now, five hundred million pairs of eyes were preparing to fixate on TV screens large or small, black-and-white or full color, full of static, with tinfoil antennas and all manner of home-remedy repairs—anything, anything! to get a glimpse of that first step on the moon. But there was this small matter of wind whipping about in Australia that, unbeknownst to eager television viewers, was threatening to put the kibosh on the broadcast altogether.

"*We got hit by a very big wind squall,*" explained Neil Mason, one of two drivers for the *Parkes Radio Telescope* during Apollo 11. "*And wind's one of the worst things that can happen with a dish because of the large connecting area. Wind blows against the dish in particular angles, and, for one thing, can burn out the drive motors.*"

Much of the world had joined America in anticipating man's first lunar steps—not just as observers, but in effort as well. And at Parkes, it was their Dish—smack in the middle of the sheep field—that would capture the signals being transmitted by a camera placed on the surface of the moon by Neil.

That camera was the first of its kind. A 7-pound, hand-held, point-and-shoot, remote, shrunken version of a conventional 400-pound studio camera. It was created over a five-year period by more than three hundred people at Westinghouse Electric. Its creation was nothing short of miraculous.

For the moonwalk to actually appear on TV, the lunar camera would first capture the image of the astronauts, then relay the image from the moon to . . . *Parkes, Australia*. Whereupon the signal would be sent (by microwave) 150 miles east to Sydney, and then across the Pacific Ocean (by satellite) to the control center in Houston. From there, the image would go out to the TV networks and then, finally, to television sets and anxious viewers throughout America and the world.

"[When] we'd encountered strong winds like that before," said Cliff Smith, mechanical foreman at Parkes, *"we didn't use the Dish. It was stowed, in an upright position, up on jacks—so no damage could be done. Our senior staff out here in Parkes didn't take risks."*

Despite the historical significance of the moon shot, Smith was fully expecting to be told by his supervisors that they were shutting down the telescope—it was that dangerous. With men stationed on top of the Dish, and inside, below it, the risks were real and the results could be deadly—should the Dish flat out collapse.

The wind gusts had surpassed double the allowable limit (they were now pounding the Dish at 70 mph), whooshing in intermittent blasts; coming in from the southwest and striking from behind. Even if the men went unharmed, a mangled telescope would be unable to snatch transmission signals traveling from the moon. And if no signals . . . then no TV . . . and no millions of witnesses to One Giant Leap.

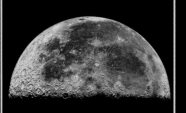

(p.40) The Parkes Radio Telescope in Australia. The Dish was designed to pick up as many radio waves as possible from a specific point in the sky (say, for instance, the moon). The system captured these very weak cosmic signals and amplified them more than a "million million times." (photo © CSIRO) (p.41) This blurred photo is the only known image of the famous windstorm at the Parkes telescope. (photo © David Cooke)

"Our gentlemen in charge must have said, 'We have to take some risks in this world and let ours be this one,'" mused Smith. "It was a special occasion, and people were depending on us—well, we thought they were."

So, amidst the biting chill of the wind, and with nerves of steel, Cliff Smith stayed at his post on top of the Dish—up on the track where all the machinery was. He (along with a partner) was ready to manually let down the huge sixty-four-meter telescope if he had to—if it would even go down. He was ready to hand-crank the behemoth if it should come to that (to keep tracking the moon signal if the motor went out).

And, amidst the incessant alarm ringing inside, Neil Mason sat at his post, a console, where, as the driver of the Dish, he—especially he—needed to stay focused on the task at hand. He was not allowed to turn his head, even for a moment, to sneak a peek at the mesmerizing images coming in on the monitor.

"I had to make sure I kept the Dish pointed where we were getting the best signal all the time," Mason recalled. "You had to have the coordinates [of the moon] to plug in and you had to concentrate on what you were doing—you couldn't just sit there and gather sleep or you'd end up in a bit of a mess."

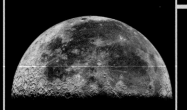

(p.42) Neil Armstrong practices with the TV camera during training exercises. (p.43) In one of the first images of man on the moon, Neil scoops up a small amount of lunar soil to bring back to Earth in case they should have to make a sudden departure from the moon. The image was captured by the 16mm film camera on the LM.

"Armstrong is on the moon. Neil Armstrong—thirty-eight-year-old American—standing on the surface of the moon!"—Walter Cronkite, television newscaster for CBS

In keeping with NASA's overall Apollo program creed of backup, backup, backup, there might have been other possibilities for getting the TV signal. In fact, Parkes had originally been scheduled as a back-up station; but a few months prior to the landing, it was moved up to the prime receiving station. Still, at the Parkes telescope, they had no way of knowing if the signals from backups Goldstone (in California) or Honeysuckle Creek (in Australia) were coming through.

"Our first signal wasn't very good for the simple reason that it was what we called an offset beam—it was only using part of the Dish," explained Cliff Smith. *"But as soon as they got it on the main focus, things changed; and that's when Sydney Video decided that our signal was the best and sent it across the world."*

The Parkes signal was of such superior quality to the other incoming signals that, other than the first few minutes (which were switched among the three telescopes), the remainder of the two-and-a-half-hour moonwalk was broadcast via Parkes.

And that ferocious wind that threatened to do in the whole show? It was outlasted and overcome by a group of cool-headed, dedicated people who were determined that the world should see—and share in the exhilaration—as man first stepped out onto the moon: facing (ironically), for the first time in history, a world *without* wind.

"Boy, look at those pictures. Wow!"—TV commentator Walter Cronkite

"It's a little shadowy; but they said they expected that in the shadow of the lunar module."—Walter Cronkite

"Well thank you television for letting us watch this one."—Astronaut Wally
Schirra, broadcasting on air with Walter Cronkite

"Isn't this something . . . two hundred forty thousand miles out there on the
moon and we're seeing this."—Walter Cronkite

Challenge 6: The Alien Environment

Before blasting off from the moon to rendezvous (or link up) with the command module and return home to Earth, the astronauts—in one of the final housekeeping chores—would fling their backpacks from the porch of the lunar module. It was a bit like tossing out the nightly trash—giving the bulky white lumps a permanent resting spot on the rocky surface. But to Neil and Buzz, the Portable Life Support System, or PLSS (pronounced *pliss*), wasn't a heap of last night's garbage. It was a pack of pure gold. It was oxygen. It was pressure. It was life.

Buzz Aldrin, from the surface of the moon: "Houston, how does our timeline appear to be going?"

CapCom, from Mission Control in Houston: "Roger: It looks like you're about [a] half hour slow on it. We're working on consumables. Over."

Dot. Dot . . . dot dot . . . dot.

That was Tom Sanzone dotting with his pencil. He was one of the PLSS engineers monitoring the backpacks from Houston, working on things like consumables—things that could be used up, or consumed—things like oxygen that the astronauts could not survive without. Oh, it was a challenge all right to get to the moon. But once they were there, the challenges didn't let up. Because the moon had no atmospheric pressure and no air to breathe. If the PLSS didn't do its job, it would be one short moonwalk. When Mission Control "worked on consumables," they were figuring out just how much time the astronauts had left outside of their spacecraft.

(p.46) Buzz Aldrin on the bottom rung of the ladder. His PLSS, which looks cumbersome on his back, along with the oxygen purge system on top, weighs only about 20 pounds on the moon. (p.47) Buzz carries the experiments out to the deployment site just south of the LM. In his right hand is the laser ranging retro-reflector experiment, and in his left hand is the passive seismic experiment (quake detector). At the end of the moonwalk, when Neil and Buzz fling their backpacks from the porch of the lunar module, the quake detector registers the impact back on Earth. It works!

The PLSS provided the astronaut with an Earth-like atmosphere in an alien environment: oxygen, pressure, ventilation. It supplied water to cool the body, and it cleansed and recycled oxygen.

From the beginning of the moonwalk, Tom Sanzone and several other PLSS engineers were plotting points on graph paper to show the rates of airflow and oxygen use, of pressure in the oxygen tank, the battery current, and changes in other critical systems.

"We took a highlighter," recalled Sanzone, an engineer for *Hamilton Standard (the contractor for the PLSS), "and we would highlight the graph paper on where we expected the data to fall. And then, if we were plotting the data, and it fell out of that point, we'd say, 'Hey! We've got a problem; or we've got something we need to look at.'"*

They had put man on the moon that day, true; but computers in 1969 barely had the computing power of today's hand-held calculators. So a lot of analysis was done the good old-fashioned way: paper, pencil, and brainpower.

The engineers monitored the astronauts closely in the mission evaluation room (MER). Any of the data falling outside their specific parameters might be cause to end the EVA (or extravehicular activity—spacespeak for moonwalk) earlier than scheduled.

"The MER . . . was in a building with separate rooms," explained Sanzone. *"For every flight controller in the front room, in Mission Control, there were rooms around the control center with that controller's backup people. The MER was the backup to the backup room. That's where the engineering directorate people and the contractors were."*

There were a number of PLSS engineers, each responsible for five or six indicators of a particular astronaut. Tom Sanzone was assigned to monitor certain data for Armstrong during the EVA. Others monitored Buzz Aldrin. No one was assigned to astronaut Mike Collins. Mike was still circling the moon—keeping the command module working so he and Neil and Buzz would be able to get back home again. He would not walk on the moon. He would not need a PLSS.

The PLSS, developed for Apollo by the Hamilton Standard Company in Connecticut (now Hamilton Sundstrand), took an estimated 2.5 million man-hours to create from conception through completion. Weighing 85 pounds on Earth and worn as a backpack, it allowed up to a four-hour moonwalk (though the *Apollo 11* mission plan called for an EVA of about 2 1/2 hours). It was a remarkably reliable piece of hardware.

"We were obviously always concerned that something could fail," engineer Tom Sanzone said. "The pump could fail, the communications could fail, the fan could fail. . . . In the portable life support system, we were not fail-operational [with a backup system], we were fail-safe. And that meant that at the first failure, you had to go to a system that would keep you alive—you had to go immediately back into the vehicle."

"Far from feeling lonely or abandoned, I feel very much a part of what is taking place on the lunar surface."—Astronaut Michael Collins

"I know that I would be a liar or a fool if I said that I have the best of the three Apollo 11 seats, but I can say with truth and equanimity that I am perfectly satisfied with the one I have."—Michael Collins

But luckily, during that historic, first-ever exploration of an alien world, all went well. The indicators that Sanzone and the other PLSS engineers were watching, such as battery voltage, carbon dioxide level, and primary oxygen system pressure—those low-tech dots they had been plotting—continued to fall within the predictable and acceptable range. The backpacks were performing superbly.

CapCom, from Houston: "We've been looking at your consumables, and you're in good shape. Subject to your concurrence, we'd like to extend the duration of the EVA one-five [15] minutes from nominal."

Neil Armstrong, from the moon: "Okay. That sounds fine."

Walk on the moon a little longer? Oh, absolutely . . . especially since those dots were all in perfect range.

At the end of the moonwalk, the mission plan called for the backpacks to be jettisoned—tossed from the lunar module. They wouldn't be needed anymore, but their stowage space would be: to bring home a few souvenirs—of the rock variety.

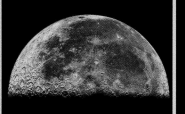

(p.48) Michael Collins, alone in the command module, circled the moon once every 2 hours while Neil and Buzz were on the surface. He maintained a communications link with Mission Control, flying solo for 28 hours before rendezvousing with the Eagle. This photo was taken by Neil and Buzz in the lunar module after the craft had first separated and the LM was just preparing to land. (p.49) Some of the precious rocks they brought back. Contrary to popular lore, the astronauts did not get to keep even one souvenir for themselves.

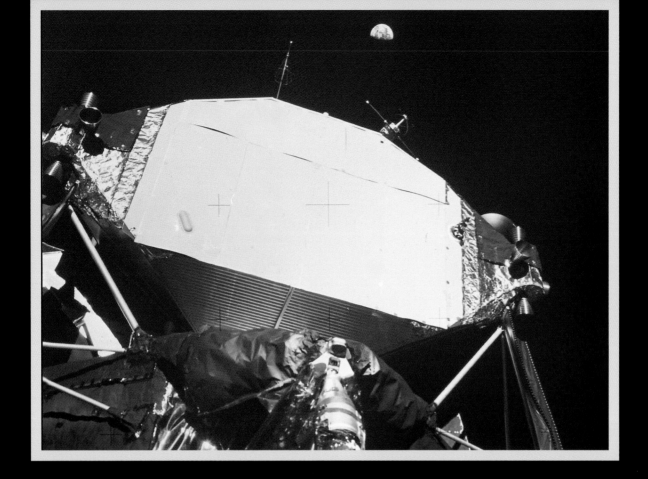

Homeward Bound . . .The Final 240,000 Miles

Moon germs. Bugs. Deadly killer bugs that would come back from the moon, spread—unstoppable—over planet Earth and Do In Humanity. That was the big worry for the *Apollo 11* homecoming. At least for some. It was man's first time ever in an alien environment and, really, who knew what to expect? Who knew what horrors lay in wait? But many thought the risk was blown out of proportion; many thought the risk completely nonexistent. After all, with no evidence of any life on the moon, why would there be killer germs?

The higher-ups at NASA, though, prodded by the Academy of Sciences, were taking no chances. Just in case, precautionary measures had been put in place: Biological isolation garments would greet, and then encase, the astronauts when they were plucked from the ocean at recovery. The astronauts would then be sealed away in isolation, quarantined (in the lunar receiving lab, or LRL) for nearly a month—with special germ-free mice. The mice were the test: If they lived, supposedly there were no moon germs and the guys went free. If they died . . . well, then, no one knew quite what would happen.

(p.50) The ascent stage of the lunar module—needed to lift the LM off the moon and boost it into lunar orbit. It was the astronauts' only ticket home to Earth. (p.51) The lunar module, after a successful liftoff from the moon, approaches *Columbia* for the critical rendezvous.

But first, the astronauts had to get off the moon. And get home. And that had everyone—from the pot scrubbers to the grand Pooh-Bahs—*everyone* worried just a bit. The ascent from the moon would be a seven-minute exercise in who could hold their breath the longest. There was one chance—one—for the engine to fire properly and lift the *Eagle* into orbit. Either it worked, or it didn't. If the engine failed midway through the burn, the LM would crash back onto the moon. If the engine failed to start altogether, there was enough oxygen to keep the astronauts alive for just one day. The ascent engine, made by Rocketdyne and Bell Aerosystems, had only four moving parts (simplicity, the thinking went, would carry them to success). And though workers at Rocketdyne were supremely confident, they would probably win the breath-holding contest nonetheless.

And then . . . ten-nine-eight . . . and they were off the moon.

This, despite the fact that, eight years before the launch, the prevailing wisdom was, as one of NASA's chief engineers, Caldwell Johnson put it, *"It just seemed absolutely out of the question to get up there and separate these craft, and one go down and one somehow launch again and meet up with the first one."* But that is exactly what happened. It happened exactly as planned, precisely on schedule. The *Eagle* and *Columbia* were able to perform a successful rendezvous, and *Apollo 11* was now able to begin the roughly quarter-million-mile journey homeward-bound.

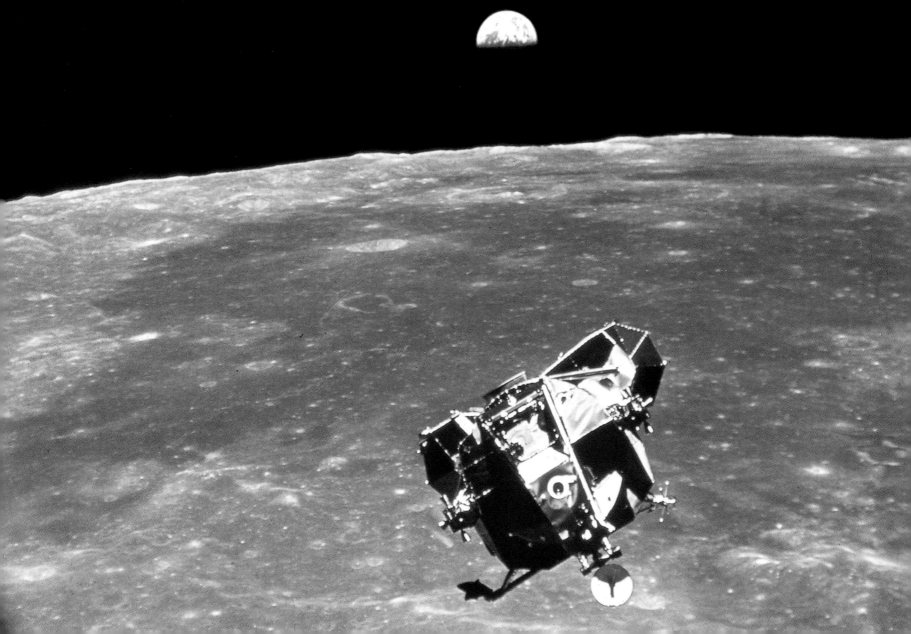

There remained, though, yet *another* hurdle near home: the fiery reentry. Home's door was a frightfully narrow corridor into Earth's atmosphere. If the command module came in too steep, it would burn up; if too shallow, it would skip out of the atmosphere forever. Even if it came in just right, traveling at 25,000 miles per hour, *Columbia* would be engulfed in a fireball when it smashed back into the atmosphere. The temperature on the outside of the spacecraft would reach 5,000 degrees. It is astounding to think that anything—let alone anyone—could survive that.

But, there was a remarkable ablative heat shield covering the capsule. Created by the Avco Corporation, three years in the making, it surrounded and protected the astronauts. The special ablative material (which absorbs and dissipates heat) was inserted meticulously by hand into an outer plastic honeycomb shell comprised of 400,000 individual cells. Four hundred thousand honeycomb cells. Interesting.

It's almost as though there was one honeycomb cell representing each person who worked on *Apollo 11*—the great team effort— 400,000 strong. It is as if those 400,000 people had come together— symbolically—at the end, at this last moment, to personally wrap a protective arm around *their* astronauts and *their* spacecraft and *their* years of effort. To bring *Apollo 11* home safely and accomplish the task they'd so boldly set out to do.

They could do this.

Challenge 7: Images and Glitches

It is said that a picture is worth a thousand words. During the Apollo program, an amendment was tacked onto that old adage, courtesy of NASA's Dick Underwood: *"Your key to immortality is solely in the quality of your photographs."*

While talking with the crew of *Apollo 11* in the final briefing before launch, Underwood, who was NASA's supervisory aerospace technician in space optics, tried to emphasize one last time what he had been telling them in training for years. When they returned from the moon they'd be heroes, have dinner at the White House, have parades, along with other hoopla. Meanwhile, computers would be compiling all sorts of data that would be stored in volume upon volume, housed in libraries, research centers, and archives, which most people would never see, would never read, would never hear about.

"But," he told them, *"if your photographs are great—they'll live forever. If someone really wants to know you went, they see your pictures."*

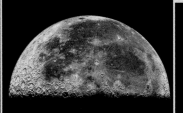

(p.52) A stunning view as *Apollo 11* approaches Earth on its return from the moon. This image was taken prior to reentry and shows a dramatic red tint near Earth's terminator. (p.53) The classic astronaut photo. Buzz Aldrin on the surface of the moon, photographed by Neil Armstrong, who is reflected in Aldrin's visor. It is NASA's most requested photo. It is one of the most recognizable images worldwide. Imagine if it didn't exist!

Underwood's photography department was charged with the task of documenting the moon missions in images. He set about modifying cameras and development processes, transforming the astronauts into regular shutterbugs. They worked closely with the Hasselblad company on the cameras and with the Kodak Company on the film and processing equipment. *Apollo 11* took three modified Hasselblad cameras to the moon: One stayed with Collins in the command module, and the other two were brought to the surface with Neil and Buzz in the lunar module.

"On the surface of the moon," explained Dick Underwood, *"they had a roll of film and no ability to change it. So the programming and training were based on 'What are you going to get in a couple hundred shots?'"*

Underwood taught the astronauts to "shoot from the hip," not using a viewfinder, the eyepiece one generally looks through on a camera. They practiced in the KC-135 aircraft—simulating zero gravity, or no gravity—for roughly thirty seconds at a time, flying parabolas (high arcs with steep drops). They practiced at home snapping photos of their kids; learning about exposure techniques and camera lens settings like f-stop and shutter and film speed. And when *Apollo 11* finally launched, Dick Underwood was confident that man's first steps on the moon would look pretty darn good.

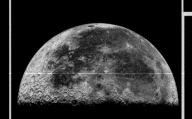

(pp.54—55) Earthrise series, photographed from the command module, in lunar orbit, after the moonwalk, with all three astronauts onboard. Astronaut Michael Collins remarked in his memoirs that Earthrise was a *"truly dramatic moment that we all scramble[d] to record with our cameras."*

Remember that in the planning stages of *Apollo 11*, a great brouhaha erupted when certain NASA personnel became obsessed with the idea of "moon bugs"—deadly germs that the astronauts might bring back from the moon and contaminate Earth with. Underwood was one who thought the idea ludicrous. But nonetheless, the enforced quarantine meant that everything that came back with the astronauts—including rocks and film—would also be locked up. The trouble, of course, was that NASA officials wanted the photos ASAP.

"Our first answer was, 'Well, it's pretty simple. You're going to let them [the astronauts] out someday. Let the film sit in there with them for a month and then we won't have to . . . jeopardize the film in any way whatsoever—just let it sit in a cold vault.' And that was the simple system," Underwood explained. *"But they said, 'Oh no, people want to see it as soon as possible after the flight.' They then decided we would have to decontaminate the film, or kill any of these bugs that might do in humanity, and get the film out."*

And so, for the next eighteen months, Underwood and a few other technicians worked on developing a reliable debugging process.

"Well, we started playing games with that, and everything we'd come up with would destroy the film," said Underwood. *"You had to come up with something that would kill all these bugs (that didn't exist in the first place) on a film, and [yet] not destroy the film. The film wasn't designed to go through that sort of thing."*

What they came up with was a process using a gaseous form of ethylene oxide. And boy was it potent . . . killed everything, even smallpox. So they were set. Mike, Neil, and Buzz were comfortable with the cameras; Dick Underwood and the technicians were trained and prepared to process the precious, priceless moon footage. Yet there was no harm in honing one's skills. And that's what photo-developing technicians Fred Southard and Terry Slezak were doing when they decided to practice again—even while *Apollo 11* was en route home from the moon.

"*[Fred Southard] took this supposed [practice] moon film, put it in the material, put it in this big container, shoved it into the autoclave, turned the system on, [went] for a break,*" recalled Dick Underwood. "*Came back, opened the door, pulled it out, and the film has melted. And they're on their way back from the moon! He comes over to the lab with this roll of film that's a clump of melted plastic at this point,* and oh my God! . . . *Called the boss and everybody. 'Hey, we have a glitch in the system.'*"

A *glitch* in the system! As Underwood pointed out, you cannot go back to the moon—not for the first time. It's either—or. You get the photos, or you don't. There are no "do-overs." It was the decontaminant, ethylene oxide, that had somehow dripped and destroyed the film. So again, Underwood said: Leave the film in quarantine with the astronauts, don't take the risk—develop it normally and don't expose the film to the hazard. But again, he was overruled by the NASA administrators.

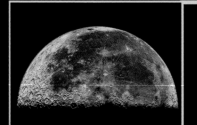

(p.56) Buzz trains with the Hasselblad camera in the KC-135 plane (used to simulate zero gravity). Notice he is not looking through any type of viewfinder. (p.57) Armstrong, Collins, and Aldrin review the photographic footage from the mission while they are in the LRL (lunar receiving lab), quarantined for a month. It is quickly discovered (by other NASA personnel) that there are no good Hasselblad images (fine quality, professional grade) of Neil Armstrong on the moon. Almost all of the high-quality photos are of Buzz. (Many years later, one image is identified as Neil working at the LM, but that is all there is save for the 16mm grainy film footage.)

So they improvised and innovated. Through adrenaline-fueled, quick-as-lightning, trial-and-error experimentation, they had identified the trouble spot where the gaseous ethylene oxide collected as a liquid and dripped, dripped, dripped onto the film. They constructed a stainless steel container that went over the roll of film, put a special material inside to circulate the gaseous ethylene oxide through, and attached a fan to circulate it away from the hazardous area.

"So there was a no-no space in that container," explained Dick Underwood. "And [developer] Terry Slezak knew exactly where it was and made sure he didn't put the film anywhere near it. Had [Fred Southard] put [the test film] somewhere else, we wouldn't have caught the problem. And had the Apollo 11 film been put where he had put that test roll—it would have melted. It sure shook things up when we saw that roll come out of there when Fred Southard brought it in the room and we were looking at this jumbled mess of polyester."

When Neil, Buzz, and Mike did return from the moon, the film canisters were whisked away, and Underwood, Southard, Slezak, and a few others began their harrowing tasks. Imaginary bugs were killed, and ever so slowly . . . ever so carefully . . . one by one the images from the moon emerged.

And at least half of the old adage, amended by Dick Underwood, held true: The astronauts *had* captured brilliant shots—their key to immortality was indeed secure. But worth a thousand words? No. Here, the pictures were almost indescribable. Two thousand words? Three thousand words? Three million . . . ? How does one describe stepping on the moon?

Challenge 8: Open Chutes

Almost home. *Apollo 11* had made it to the moon: The *Eagle* had not crashed onto the surface, not become stranded there forever, and had found its way back to *Columbia*. And now, *Columbia* had found its way back to Earth, with all three astronauts onboard—whiskered and weary—but happy campers nonetheless. They were ready to make that final push (through Earth's atmosphere) and take that final plunge (into the waiting waters of the Pacific), and then announce to the world: mission accomplished.

During the voyage itself, NASA aerospace engineer Kirby Hinson's role was limited. Basically, he stood on the sidelines and crossed his fingers. But now, during this final phase, the fruits of his many years of labor would be on display. Because now it was contractors Northrop Ventura and North American—along with a small group at NASA, most of whom were in Kirby Hinson's Atmospheric Descent Systems Section—who held the astronauts' very lives in their hands.

For it was their parachute system that had to deploy exactly the right way, at exactly the right time, in order to slow down the barreling space capsule and prevent it from smacking the water at a velocity that would kill on impact.

"We always deploy three chutes," explained Kirby Hinson. "If all goes well, you come down slowly. If you lose a chute, you hit the water at what's called design velocity. Only two [chutes] are needed to safely bring [the command module] down. To see all three chutes is just like Heaven."

(p.58) This is a view of *Apollo 13*. No pictures of the *Apollo 11* parachute deployment exist. They were scheduled to land about ten minutes prior to sunrise. The weather conditions were cloudy. And they came in about thirteen miles away from the recovery ship. These three circumstances did not combine for a picture-perfect splashdown. (p.59) A view of *Apollo 12*. The splashdown site for *Apollo 11* was changed at the last minute. Thunderstorms were predicted in the area, and there was a concern that the turbulence caused by the storms could structurally damage the spacecraft.

Using three parachutes instead of just one is a complex landing solution known as clustering. It's necessary when dealing with heavier payloads, as *Apollo 11* was. But as one chute becomes two and two become three, problems begin to stack up. It is simply more difficult to cleanly deploy (or release and open) three parachutes. More difficult to deploy the chutes without resulting in entanglement; without resulting in friction (nylon chutes rubbing together), which can cause burning.

The problems of entanglement and friction could be lessened by packing the three chutes into compartments of one deployment bag, or by tying three individual deployment bags together. But if one chute got jammed in its compartment or bag . . .

"We were afraid to tie the bags together (in an effort to avoid the rubbing of nylon)," explained Kirby Hinson, "because of a fear that if one chute got caught in its bag, it could stop all of them. So we put a pilot parachute on each bag. Pilot parachutes fired out cannon-like, simultaneously, and then they inflated and pulled each of the main parachutes off deck [from the command module] individually."

Pilot parachutes were small (about seven feet in diameter) and inflated about fifty-eight feet above the main chutes. So on Apollo, to minimize tangling and friction-burning between the pilot and the main chutes, they used individual mortars to fire the pilot parachutes out at ninety-degree angles—one this way, one that way. By the time air drag swung them back around behind the command module, they would already be puffing up with air, and tangling would be less likely.

Then Hinson and the others had to solve the "cluster interference problem." Imagine one chute beginning to fill first with air (the ideal is for all chutes to fill simultaneously). It thereby assumes a superior position directly behind the command module while forcing the other two chutes off center. This is problematic because higher forces are now acting on that lead chute. To withstand those forces, engineers had to make a much stronger parachute than otherwise necessary. Cluster interference was certainly the most time-consuming of all their difficulties, but of course there were other problems. So they tested, tested, and retested their system until they were as confident as they could be. They stood in wind tunnels, threw boilerplate space capsules out of airplanes, threw themselves out of a perfectly good helicopter.

"We decided if we were going to ask other people to rely on any part of our work," recalled Hinson, *"we should prove that we were willing to expose ourselves to many of the same risks."*

They were confident. The system would work. They hoped.

And now *Apollo 11* was almost home . . .

(p.60) A view of *Apollo 16*. For a little more than three minutes after the command module hit Earth's atmosphere, the intense heat caused a communications blackout. The world would have to wait in silence to see if the CM had survived the fiery reentry. (p.61) A view of *Apollo 16*. On a gray morning, three 83.5-foot Ringsail parachutes opened at about 10,000 feet. The command module was eased down at a gentle 22 mph into the Pacific Ocean, about 906 statute miles from Pearl Harbor, Hawaii. All three astronauts were plucked safely from the water, hoisted onboard a helicopter, and carried to the recovery ship, the USS *Hornet*. The world breathed a sigh of relief. And rejoiced.

After sitting atop a virtual bomb and traveling nearly half a million miles; after battling 1202 alarms, low fuel, and frozen fuel slugs; after walking on an airless rock; after surviving the radiation and micrometeoroids and uncertainties of space; after a flaming reentry into the atmosphere—one would think that the risks of the mission had safely been overcome. But no.

Even after all that, it wasn't over until the end of the end.

Eight days, three hours, and eighteen minutes since it blasted out of our world, *Apollo 11* skipped back into our sky. Its silver body shimmered against the foreign backdrop of gray-blue. There was nothing Kirby Hinson nor any of the other engineers could do now but watch as gravity reintroduced itself and slammed the twelve-thousand-pound cone toward the ground. They could cross their fingers. And they did.

400,000 feet.

300,000 feet.

200,000 feet.

100,000 feet.

There is color in the sky now: orange and white, orange and white, orange and white.
Looks just like Heaven.

" *I believe this nation should commit itself to achieving the goal, before this decade is out, of landing a man on the moon and returning him safely to earth.* "

John F. Kennedy

to Congress

May 1961

"We would like to give a special thanks to all those Americans who built the spacecraft; who did the construction, design, the tests, and put their . . . hearts and all their abilities into those craft. To those people, tonight, we give a special thank you, and to all the other people that are listening and watching tonight, God bless you. Good night from Apollo 11."

—Astronaut Neil Armstrong, the day before the Earth landing, in a televised address from space

Author's Note

When writing a story of 400,000 people, questions loom: Where to begin? With whom? Who goes in? Who has to come out? Some names are so big within NASA and the space industry that it seems downright blasphemous not to mention them: James Webb, Bill Tindall, Bob Gilruth, George Low, Christopher Kraft, George Mueller, Max Faget, Wernher von Braun, Guenter Wendt, Joe Gavin and Tom Kelly at Grumman, Lee Atwood at North American . . . the list goes on. And what about all the companies and universities involved? There were literally thousands of them—large and small—yet only a few are mentioned here, because a book can only be so long.

Perhaps the inclusion-exclusion problem was best expressed by the astronauts themselves. With magnanimous grace, they chose not to list their names on the design of their mission patch—an astronaut tradition—because *Apollo 11*, the first moon landing, belonged to all.

It is critical to point out that *Apollo 11* was part of an incremental, comprehensive manned space program that began with Mercury, was then rolled into the Gemini program, and then into Apollo by the 1960s. It was made possible only by the knowledge gained from each of those missions. By the time of the *Apollo 11* liftoff, *Apollos 7, 8, 9,* and *10* (in a series of steps, with *Apollo 8* being the first to travel to the moon) had tested out the spacecraft and all of the maneuvers—everything just short of actually plunking down on the surface—that would need to be performed to accomplish the landing. Nearly everyone who worked on *Apollo 11* had worked on previous Apollo missions, and most of them would continue on with *Apollo 12.*

The stories herein are but snapshots. Just a handful of players pulled from the bench of the greatest team ever. Just a few of the 400,000 people (imagine about ten large stadiums full of fans) who set out to do an impossible task: to land man on the moon and return him safely home.

The *Apollo 11* mission patch. The astronauts wanted the image on the patch to be symbolic. They chose the bald eagle, its landing gear extended, not only for the obvious connection to the lunar module *Eagle*, but also because the eagle is a proud symbol of the United States of America. They also wanted to symbolize the peaceful nature of the mission, and so the eagle carries an olive branch—a symbol of peace.

"The fact that the little guy, no matter where he was, was part of the team and his voice got heard, I think that was the very heart and soul and strength of why the program was so successful." —Robert Carlton (CONTROL) NASA (oral history)

"I got to see firsthand the many, many, many thousands of people—and get more of a picture of how many people were dedicated—and I can't emphasize too much the word dedicated—to this program, and this job—to get a man on the moon, and get him back safely. That's what it was all about. When they lifted off and came home and they landed and picked them up, I just had such a great sense of accomplishment— not so much for myself, but for the team." —Richard Ellis, ILC Dover suit tester

"I didn't know what was going to happen that day. It started out like a day's work and blossomed into something better. I was sure proud to be there. Proud to be part of it."
—Cliff Smith, Parkes Radio Telescope, Australia

"In this expedition, everybody wanted to do the best. You didn't want to be responsible when something didn't work. If everybody took care of his part of the problem, everything would work—because they thought of everything they could."

—John Coursen, Grumman engineering manager

"Remembering being a part of the Apollo team and participating in the history-making events of the program will always bring back the pride, disappointments, sorrow, and passion shared between all of us: from the secretaries and technicians, to the astronauts and managers. For me, that was the time in history and the event to participate in above all others."

—Charlie Mars, chief LM project engineer at KSC

"It was a very historical moment, you know, the first time man's walked on the moon. You kept it on the track [the radio telescope]. It would work out. There were twenty-two people around—plenty of people in back; so we were quite confident. We knew we could do our part."

—Neil "Fox" Mason, Parkes Radio Telescope, Australia

"Well, President Kennedy wanted to be first on the moon, and all the ladies were very tuned in to that. Everyone was very proud of what they were doing, and everyone pulled their own weight—and if they had to, they would pull a little of someone else's. We wanted to get it done, and we were happy and proud to be there."

—Eleanor Foracker, ILC Dover seamstress

"I saw on a daily basis nothing but total dedication and a 100 percent work effort by all members of the workforce—from the highest-ranking NASA and contractor officials to the working levels of the combined government and private industry teams of personnel. I felt honored to be a small part of the Apollo program and at the same time extremely proud to be an American."—Ernie Reyes, chief of the Pre-flight Operations Branch

"I feel so fortunate to have been able to play a small role in what will be remembered by most as mankind's crowning achievement of the twentieth century. The thing that we on the NASA team all felt, and on a daily basis, was that each and every one of us was helping to make history. The 'Spirit of Apollo' is still something you hear mentioned around NASA, more than a third of a century later. The essence of that spirit was embodied in the dedication and focus of the team."—Tom Sanzone, PLSS engineer, Hamilton Standard

"The ultimate 'Team Moon' was probably the American public. There was almost total support for the lunar landing effort, and that support was palpable to the smaller team lucky enough to be doing the work. We were energized by, and grateful for, that support."

—Kirby Hinson, parachute recovery systems

"The lunar module was a team effort: NASA, Grumman, its subcontractors. None of us will forget being members of that team."

—Joe Gavin, vice president, Grumman Aerospace Corporation

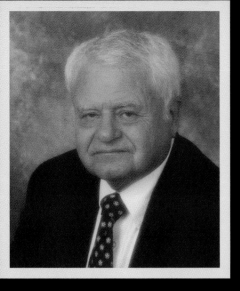

"To be a full-fledged member of the Apollo 11 *Lunar Team* meant that everyone (planners, builders, engineers, flight controllers, trainers, etc.) was well aware that the excellent photography would be, in the long run, mankind's main connection with the greatest event in human history."

—Richard Underwood, chief of photography

"We were all very young, very eager, very excited, and probably most of all, totally awed by the adventure that we found ourselves in. I don't think any of us really understood quite how we got to be there—and I think most of us had that very strong feeling of camaraderie, or partnership, or team. We knew darn well that each of us was a very, very small part of a huge jigsaw puzzle that the country was trying desperately to put together 'before the end of the decade.' We each had evolved to some small part in the whole, and knew it, and depended on each other, sometimes without even realizing it. I guess that's what being part of an effective team is all about."

—Jack Garman, Apollo Guidance Computer Support,
Mission Control

"Those were thrilling times. Too many highlights to name just one. And anxious moments . . . with Apollo 11, I thought they'd never put that thing down [land the LM] . . . they just kept going and going. But for me, the greatest thing was that my daughters [were able to] share in [the] Apollo program with me."

—Max Faget, NASA chief engineer

Sources

Tape-recorded interviews with the author:

John Coursen (March 2004), Richard Ellis (March 2004), Max Faget (April 2004), Eleanor Foracker (March 2004), Jack Garman (April 2004), Joseph Gavin (March 2004), Kirby Hinson (April 2004), Charlie Mars (February 2004), Neil Mason (March 2004), James McBarron (March 2004), Ernie Reyes (September 2004), Tom Sanzone (February 2004), Emil Schiesser (March 2004), Cliff Smith (March 2004), Richard Underwood (March 2004), Ron Woods (April 2004)

Apollo 11 mission transcripts. NASA, July 16—24, 1969.

Apollo 11 press kit. NASA, 1969.

Apollo Lunar Surface Journal online: www.hq.nasa.gov/office/pao/History/alsj/

Armstrong, Neil, Michael Collins, and Edwin E. Aldrin Jr., with Gene Farmer and Dora Jane Hamblin. *First on the Moon.* New York: Little, Brown and Company, 1970; special edition Easton Press, 1999.

Brooks, Courtney G., James M. Grimwood, and Loyd S. Swenson. *Chariots for Apollo: A History of Manned Lunar Spacecraft.* NASA History Series, SP-4205, 1979.

Carlton, Robert. Oral history transcript, NASA Johnson Space Center Oral History Project. Interviewed by Kevin M. Rusnak, Houston, Tex., April 10, 2001.

Chaikin, Andrew. *A Man on the Moon.* New York: Penguin Books USA, 1994; special edition Easton Press, 1999.

Collins, Michael. *Carrying the Fire: An Astronaut's Journeys.* New York: Farrar, Straus and Giroux, 1974. Used with permission of Farrar, Straus and Giroux.

Cortright, Edgar M., ed. *Apollo Expeditions to the Moon.* NASA History Series, SP-350, 1975.

Cronkite, Walter, with Wally Schirra. Newscast. © 1969 CBS Worldwide Inc. All rights reserved. Originally broadcast on the *CBS Evening News* on July 20, 1969, over the CBS Television Network. Used with permission of CBS.

Garman, John (Jack) R. Oral history transcript, NASA Johnson Space Center Oral History Project. Interviewed by Kevin M. Rusnak, Houston, Tex., March 27, 2001.

Hamilton Standard Press Releases, 1969. NASA archives. Brochures and press releases.

Hinson, James (Kirby). Oral history transcript, NASA Johnson Space Center Oral History Project. Interviewed by Kevin M. Rusnak, Louisburg, N.C., May 2, 2000.

Johnson, Caldwell C. Oral history transcript, NASA Johnson Space Center Oral History Project. Interviewed by Michelle Kelly, League City, Tex., April 1, 1998.

Kennedy, John F. Speech before a joint session of Congress. Washington, D.C., May 1961.

Kranz, Gene. *Failure Is Not an Option*. New York: Simon & Schuster, 2000. Used with permission of Simon & Schuster Adult Publishing Group.

McBarron, James. Oral history transcript, NASA Johnson Space Center Oral History Project. Interviewed by Kevin M. Rusnak, Frederica, Del., April 10, 2000.

Mission Control audiotapes. Apollo 11. NASA, July 20, 1969.

NASA History Archives, Washington, D.C.

NASA Online History Division: www.hq.nasa.gov/office/pao/History/apollo.html

NASA Press Release No. 69-83-K. July 6, 1969, NASA History Archives.

The Project Apollo Archive and the Apollo Image Gallery online: www.apolloarchive.com/apollo_archive.html

Safire, William. Untitled speech (together with memo titled "In Event of Moon Disaster," author unknown), Nixon Presidential Materials Staff. White House Special Files [WHSF]. Staff Member Office Files [SMOF]. H. R. Haldeman, Box 294, Folder [H. R. Haldeman Personnel Material], National Archives and Records Administration.

Swanson, Glen E., ed. *"Before This Decade Is Out . . ." Personal Reflections on the Apollo Program*. NASA History Series, NASA SP-4223, 1999.

Underwood, Richard W. Oral history transcript, NASA Johnson Space Center Oral History Project. Interviewed by Summer Chick Bergen, Houston, Tex., October 17, 2000.

Chapter Notes

And Upward . . .
"The Countdown Demonstration Test, or CDDT . . ." Reyes, interview.

Maiden Voyage . . .The Final 10 Miles
"The Eagle has wings!" Armstrong, mission transcripts.

"Today is not the day to get stuck in an elevator." Kranz, Failure Is Not an Option.

"In the next hour we will do something . . ." Kranz, Failure Is Not an Option.

"You are Go for PDI." CapCom, mission transcripts.

Challenge 1: Alarms
"Program alarm. It's a 1202." Armstrong, mission transcripts.

"1202." Aldrin, mission transcripts.

"It's the same one we had [in the simulator]." CapCom Duke, audiotapes.

"And so, [Flight Director] Gene Kranz, who's the real hero . . ." Garman, interview.

"So I remember going back to my little corner . . ." Garman, interview.

"Give us a reading on the 1202 program alarm." Armstrong, mission transcripts.

"The astronauts had no idea what these alarms were . . ." Garman, interview.

"We are Go on that alarm." CapCom Duke, mission transcripts.

"Program alarm! Same one." Aldrin, mission transcripts.

"CapCom, we are Go for landing." Kranz, mission transcripts.

"Program alarm. 1201." Aldrin, mission transcripts.

"When it occurred again a few minutes later . . ." Garman, oral history.

"Roger, no sweat." CapCom, audiotapes.

Challenge 2: Almost Empty
"Sixty Seconds!" CapCom Duke, mission transcripts.

"We wanted to give him [Neil] every chance to land . . ." Carlton, oral history.

"I never dreamed we would still be flying . . ." Kranz, Failure Is Not an Option.

"When we tripped low level . . ." Carlton, oral history.

Landing Spread
"People [were] concerned about the amount of fuel you had left . . ." Mars, interview.

"Forty feet, down two and a half . . ." Aldrin, mission transcripts.

"You know it's real when you walk [into the Mission Control building] . . ." Garman, interview.

"Houston, Tranquility Base here . . ." Armstrong, mission transcripts.

"Roger, Tranquility. We copy you on the ground . . ." CapCom Duke, mission transcripts.

"I was so excited, I couldn't get out Tranquility . . ." CapCom Duke, "Before This Decade Is Out . . ."

Challenge 3: Frozen Slug
"You know, they landed, and everybody's cheering . . ." Coursen, interview.

"First thing we did was get the drawings out so you could see . . ." Coursen, interview.

Challenge 4: First Steps
"I'm going to step off the LM now." Armstrong, mission transcripts.

"That's one small step for man, one giant leap for mankind." Armstrong, mission transcripts.

"The design goal of the space suit was to give man enough mobility . . ." Ellis, interview.

"Reaching down is fairly easy." Aldrin, mission transcripts.

"The space suit in itself is probably a little more than half engineering and the rest art . . ." McBarron, interview.

"I would just put the suit on, become pressurized . . ." Ellis, interview.

"Traction seems quite good." Aldrin, mission transcripts.

"People don't realize one of the few pieces of equipment that . . . had to work . . ." McBarron, oral history.

"It's absolutely no trouble to walk around." Armstrong, mission transcripts.

"We made up each layer separately for the whole suit . . ." Foracker, interview.

"The so-called kangaroo hop does work . . ." Aldrin, mission transcripts.

"I approved the design of the lunar boots . . ." McBarron, interview.

"I spent a lot of time walking on a treadmill . . ." Ellis, interview.

"When it came time you had a problem that needed to be worked . . ." McBarron, interview.

"I noticed in the soft spots where we have . . ." Armstrong, mission transcripts.

"Like our president said, 'We didn't worry too much until the guys on the moon started jumping . . .'" Foracker, interview.

Challenge 5: Wind

"We got hit by a very big wind squall . . ." Mason, interview.

"[When] we'd encountered strong winds like that before . . ." Smith, interview.

"Our gentlemen in charge must have said, 'We have to take some risks . . .'" Smith, interview.

"I had to make sure I kept the Dish pointed where we were getting the best signal . . ." Mason, interview.

"Armstrong is on the moon . . ." Cronkite, *CBS Evening News*.

"Our first signal wasn't very good for the simple reason that it was . . ." Smith, interview.

"Boy, look at those pictures. Wow!" . . . Cronkite, *CBS Evening News*.

"It's a little shadowy; but they said they expected . . ." Cronkite, *CBS Evening News*.

"Well thank you television for letting us watch this one." Schirra, *CBS Evening News*.

"Isn't this something . . . two-hundred forty thousand miles out there . . ." Cronkite, *CBS Evening News*.

Challenge 6: The Alien Environment

"Houston, how does our timeline appear to be going?" Aldrin, mission transcripts.

"Roger: It looks like you're about [a] half hour slow on it . . ." CapCom, mission transcripts.

"We took a highlighter, and we would highlight the graph paper . . ." Sanzone, interview.

"The MER . . . was in a building with separate rooms . . ." Sanzone, interview.

"We're obviously always concerned that something could fail . . ." Sanzone, interview.

"Far from feeling lonely or abandoned, I feel very much a part of what is taking place on the lunar surface." Collins, *Carrying the Fire*.

"I know that I would be a liar or a fool if I said that I have the best of the three Apollo 11 seats . . ." Collins, *Carrying the Fire*.

"We've been looking at your consumables . . ." CapCom, mission transcripts.

"Okay. That sounds fine." Armstrong, mission transcripts.

Homeward Bound . . . The Final 240,000 Miles

"It just seemed absolutely out of the question to get up there and separate these craft . . ." Johnson, oral history.

Challenge 7: Images and Glitches

"Your key to immortality is solely in the quality of your photographs." Underwood, interview.

"But if your photographs are great—they'll live forever . . ." Underwood, interview.

"On the surface of the moon, they had a roll of film and no ability to change it . . ." Underwood, interview.

"[T]ruly dramatic moment that we all scramble[d] to record . . ." Collins, *Carrying the Fire*.

"*Our first answer was, 'Well, it's pretty simple.'* . . ." Underwood, interview.

"*Well, we started playing games with that* . . ." Underwood, interview.

"*[Fred Southard] took this supposed [practice] moon film, put it in the material* . . ." Underwood, oral history.

"*So there was a no-no space in that container* . . ." Underwood, interview.

Challenge 8: Open Chutes

"*We always deploy three chutes* . . ." Hinson, interview.

"*We were afraid to tie the bags together* . . ." Hinson, interview.

"*We decided if we were going to ask other people to rely on* . . ." Hinson, interview.

Final Spread

"*We would like to give a special thanks to all those Americans who built the spacecraft* . . ." Armstrong, mission transcripts.

Additional Sources Consulted

Books:

Godwin, Robert, ed. *Apollo 11: The NASA Mission Reports, volumes 1–3*. Compiled from the NASA archives. Apogee Books, 1971. / Kelly, Thomas J. *Moon Lander: How We Developed the Apollo Lunar Module*. Washington: Smithsonian Institution Press, 2001. / Kraft, Chris. *Flight: My Life in Mission Control*. New York: Penguin, 2001. / Lay, Beirne, Jr. *Earthbound Astronauts: The Builders of the Apollo-Saturn*. New Jersey: Prentice-Hall, 1971. / Light, Michael. *Full Moon*. New York: Knopf, 1999. / Mailer, Norman. *Of a Fire on the Moon*. New York: Signet, 1969. / Murray, Charles, and Catherine Bly Cox. *Apollo: The Race to Moon*. New York: Simon & Schuster, 1989. / Pellegrino, Charles R., and Joshua Stoff. *Chariots for Apollo: The Untold Story Behind the Race to the Moon*. New York: Avon Books, 1985. / Reynolds, David West. *Apollo: The Epic Journey to the Moon*. New York: Tehabi Books, Harcourt, 2002.

Oral History Transcripts:

Johnson Space Center Oral History Project. Interview transcripts of the following: Neil Armstrong, Dr. Charles A. Berry (aerospace medicine), Michael Collins, Max Faget, Jay Honeycutt (simulator supervisor), Thomas Kelly (Grumman lunar module), John Kiker (parachutes), Joe Schmidt (lead suit technician), John Stonesifier (recovery operations), Guenter Wendt (pad leader).

NASA Special Materials and Miscellany:

AP wire reports, NASA archives. / Compton, William David. *Where No Man Has Gone Before: A History of Apollo Lunar Exploration Missions*. NASA History Series; NASA SP-4214. / Johnson, Caldwell, NASA engineer. Interview by Don Neff of Time Inc., Houston bureau. Marshall Space Center, February 7, 1969; Houbolt file, NASA archives. / Kennedy Space Center news release KSC-330-69. NASA archives, Sherrod files, Apollo 11 box. / Front Page World Papers; NASA Headquarters History Office archives, Washington, D.C. Apollo 11 general folder 7354. / NASA SP-4104 "NASA Engineers and the Age of Apollo." / Press release Avco Corporation. Brochures and press releases; NASA archives, folder 7285. / Robert Sherrod (journalist) Files, NASA history archives. / Tomayko, James E. "Computers in Spaceflight: The NASA Experience." NASA History Office. NASA contractor report 182505; contract NASW-3714. Wichita State University, Kansas, March 1988. / Wendt, Guenter, pad leader. Interview conducted by Grimwood and Ertel, May 23, 1967 (location of interview unknown); NASA archives.

Technical Reports, Catalogues, and Miscellany:

Arnold, H.J.P. *Lunar Surface Photography: A Study of Apollo 11.* Abstract. I.A.F. Congress, October 10–17, 1987; paper no. IAA-87-646; Space Frontiers Limited; NASA archives, impact photography, folder 6579. / Fleisig, Ross. "The First Manned Lunar Landing Spacecraft." 45th Congress of the International Astronautical Federation. Jerusalum, Israel, October 9–14, 1994. NASA archives general files, folder 7277; Apollo 11 (AS 506) general. / "Fly Me to the Moon." An interview with Joseph G. Gavin Jr. Technology Review. July 1994. / Gavin, Joseph, Jr. "The Apollo Lunar Module (LM): A Retrospective." 53rd International Astronautical Congress. The World Space Congress 2002; Houston, Tex., October 10–19, 2002. / Hamilton Sundstrand Portable Life Support & Space Suit Experience. HS Space Hardware; Heritage Team Report; SHH-R-002 Rev. B. / Hamilton Sundstrand (HS) Space Suit Experience Supplement. HS Space Hardware; Heritage Report; SHH-R-004 Rev. A. / *Lessons of the Lenses: The Retrospectives of Richard Underwood.* Voyage to the Future. pp. 90–94. NASA archive folder 6579. / *Managing the Moon Program: Lessons Learned from Project Apollo.* Monographs in Aerospace History No. 14, July 1999. / Platoff, Ann M. "Where No Flag Has Gone Before: Political and Technical Aspects of Placing a Flag on the Moon." Hernandez Engineering Inc., Houston. NASA Contractor Report 188251. JSC History Portal. / TWA news release. NASA archives; Apollo 11 brochures and releases, folder 7285.

Online and Multimedia:

Apollo 11: Men on the Moon. DVD. Spacecraft Films. Charlotte: Red Pepper Creative, 2002; 20th Century Fox Home Entertainment Inc., 2003. / "Apollo 11: I Remember." MSNBC TV News online: www.msnbc.com/onair/msnbc/TimeAndAgain/archive/apollo/remember.asp / The Apollo Program. Smithsonian online: www.nasm.si.edu/collections/imagery/apollo/apollo.htm / The ApolloSaturn Reference Page: www.apollosaturn.com / Biography of Dr. Wernher von Braun. Marshall Space Flight Center, Huntsville, Alabama: history.msfc.nasa.gov/vonbraun/index.html / "CSM Parachute." Encyclopedia Astronautica. www.astronautix.com / "Dateline Moon; The Media and the Space Race." Newseum. www.newseum.org/datelinemoon/ / "The Dish." Episode 16, Dimensions in Time, broadcast 6:30 P.M. on May 27, 2002: www.abc.net.au/dimensions/dimensions_in_time/Transcripts/s566290.htm / The First Lunar Landing: www.hq.nasa.gov/office/pao/History/ap11ann/FirstLunarLanding/toc.html / *From the Earth to the Moon.* DVD. A Clavius Base/Imagine Entertainment Production. Executive producer Tom Hanks. Producers Brian Grazer, Ron Howard, Michael Bostick. HBO Home Video, a division of Time Warner, 1998. / The Lunar Module Computer: www.abc.net.au/science/moon/computer.htm / NASA Apollo 11 30th Anniversary: www.hq.nasa.gov/office/pao/History/ap11ann/introduction.htm / Project Apollo: http://science.ksc.nasa.gov/history/apollo/apollo.html / "Reliability and Training" and "Earth Landing": ApolloSaturn.com / Sarkissian, John. *On Eagle's Wings: The Parkes Observatory's Support of the Apollo 11 Mission.* Report, October 2000: www.parkes.atnf.csiro.au/apollo11/ / Smithsonian National Air and Space Museum: http:www.nasm.si.edu / "Boeing Celebrates Apollo 11 30th Anniversary": www.boeing.com/news/feature/apollo11/index.html / SpaceAholic.com: www.spaceaholic.com/us_artifacts.htm / "To the Moon." Interview with Max Faget. Nova: www.pbs.org/wgbh/nova/tothemoon/faget.html

Acknowledgments

John Hargenrader, NASA history office archives; Bill Larsen, JSC archives; Elaine Liston, KSC archives; Gloria Sanchez, JSC media resources; Gwen Pitman, NASA imaging branch; Bert Ulrich, NASA imaging branch; Larry Feliu, Grumman History Center; Bill Ayrey, ILC Dover; Kent Carter, National Archives, Fort Worth; Rebecca Wright, NASA, JSC Oral History Project; Benny Cheney, NASA media resources; Connie Moore, NASA headquarters imaging branch; Jody Russell, JSC media resources; Kathie Muncy, Houston Photo Imaging; Margaret Persinger, KSC imaging branch; Jane Odom, NASA history archives; John Sarkissian, Parkes Observatory; Marci Brennan, Corbis; Lydia Zelaya, Simon &

Schuster; Victoria Fox, Farrar, Straus and Giroux; Eric Jones and the *Apollo Lunar Surface Journal;* Kipp Teague and the Project Apollo Archive; Andrew Chaikin, author, Apollo expert; Mike Martucci, filmmaker; Kathryn Sermak, Buzz Aldrin Organization; Ulli Lotzmann, photographer; Don Holmquist, former astronaut; Bob Carlton, Apollo mission controller; Emil Schiesser, Apollo navigation; Ron Woods, Apollo suit technician; Ann Faget (daughter of Max); and interview subjects: Joe Gavin, Kirby Hinson, Dick Underwood, Tom Sanzone, John Coursen, Cliff Smith, Neil "Fox" Mason, Jack Garman, Richard Ellis, James McBarron, Eleanor Foracker, Charlie Mars, Ernie Reyes, and Max Faget.

A special word of thanks to Don Holmquist and Bob Carlton for reading the book in manuscript form; and to Andy Chaikin for reading it in galley form.

And last I would like to acknowledge my magnificent editor, Ann Rider, and all of Team Houghton who consistently pull together to produce many of the best books published for children today.

Photo Credits

All photos courtesy of NASA, with the following exceptions: p.4) Grumman History Center © / p.5) Corbis, U1638716 © / p.6) AP/Wide World Photos © / p.24) copyright Ulrich Lotzmann © / p.25) copyright Ulrich Lotzmann © / p.40) copyright CSIRO © / p.41) copyright David Cooke © / p.66) Cliff Smith; Richard Ellis, courtesy ILC Dover; Robert Carlton / p.67) Charlie Mars; Eleanor Foracker; John Coursen, courtesy Grumman; Neil Mason / p.68) Ernie Reyes, courtesy NASA; Joe Gavin; Kirby Hinson; Tom Sanzone / p.69) Jack Garman (with Chris Kraft); Max Faget, courtesy NASA; Richard Underwood.

For Further Exploration:

NASA Apollo 11 30th Anniversary online: www.hq.nasa.gov/office/pao/History/ap11ann/introduction.htm
An entire Web site devoted to Apollo 11 *history, facts, photos. Complete with astronaut interviews, biographies, time lines, key documents, and links to other sites.*

Apollo Lunar Surface Journal online: www.hq.nasa.gov/office/pao/History/alsj/
The most comprehensive Web site (and general resource) for all things Apollo—for all the missions. An amazing repository containing all the mission transcripts (with comments from the astronauts and the editors of the journal), NASA interviews with the astronauts, press kits, photos, videos and movies, mission reports, commentary, analysis, and more. Described by astronaut Neil Armstrong as a "living document," it is a treasure not to be missed. It is designed with adults in mind (and with lots of technical information) but easy to navigate—so you'll find plenty to discover and understand. A veritable treasure-trove.

The Project Apollo Archive and the Apollo Image Gallery online
www.apolloarchive.com/apollo_archive.html
A fantastic companion site to the Surface Journal. *This has a large number of the photographic images of the Apollo missions, complete with detailed descriptions. Includes low- and high-resolution scans. Perfect for finding an awesome photo for your computer wallpaper. Also includes mission chronology in photos and objectives/accomplishments, maps and diagrams, memorabilia, books, DVDs, and more.*

From the Earth to the Moon. DVD. A Clavius Base/Imagine Entertainment Production. Executive producer Tom Hanks. Producers Brian Grazer, Ron Howard, Michael Bostick. HBO Home Video, a division of Time Warner, 1998. *A remarkable and utterly engrossing epic miniseries hosted by Tom Hanks in cooperation with NASA. In twelve episodes, the series sets out to tell the history of the Apollo space program. With Hollywood flair, each segment* is a minimovie—self-contained, factual, and amazingly realistic. A lot of behind-the-scenes stories are revealed, and some of the thousands of nonastronauts are also featured.

Apollo 11: Men on the Moon. DVD. Spacecraft films. Charlotte: Red Pepper Creative, 2002; 20th Century Fox
Home Entertainment Inc., 2003.
More than ten hours of Apollo 11 footage on three discs, from launch to landing. Features all the onboard TV transmissions from the astronauts, all the 16mm onboard film, multiangle views of the launch and of the landing, and multiple audio tracks (including air-to-ground communications). Includes many bonus features.

The Buzz Aldrin Web site: www.buzzaldrin.com
The personal Web site of Apollo 11 astronaut Buzz Aldrin. Includes a biography, available services (speaking engagements, etc.), articles and interviews, photographs, merchandise (including a Buzz action figure and autographs), and books (including a children's book: Reaching for the Moon).

Explore the other Apollo missions that TEAM MOON made possible:

Apollo 1: The first planned manned Apollo mission. The crew was tragically killed in a fire on the launch pad while training in the command module on January 27, 1967.

Apollo 7: The first manned mission. Apollo 7 was to orbit Earth for a full eleven days, proving the capabilities and endurance of the command module. Mission Control repeatedly sent up unscheduled requests for experiments and additional duties, causing the astronauts to openly revolt and refuse commands. Commander Wally Schirra remarked: "I'm saying at this point, television will be delayed, without further discussion." This did not sit well with Houston.

Apollo 8: The first flight to orbit the moon. Apollo 8 orbited the moon on Christmas Eve 1968, and from 240,000 miles the crew radioed back to Earth a reading from the Book of Genesis: "In the beginning, God created the Heaven and the Earth . . ." They are the first crew to witness the spectacular vision of an Earthrise.

Apollo 9: Tested the lunar module in Earth orbit: all the flight maneuvers, the docking, separation, and, of course, the critical rendezvous with the command module.

Apollo 10: The dress rehearsal for the lunar landing—flying the same orbital path as Apollo 11 would, under the same lighting conditions. They flew the LM to within 50,000 feet of the surface of the moon. Astronaut Gene Cernan radioed Houston: "Oh, we are low. We are close, babe. We is down among 'em, Charlie."

Apollo 12: The goal was to achieve a pinpoint landing in the Ocean of Storms. Apollo 12 was struck by two lightning bolts at launch that tripped nearly all the circuit breakers in the command module—but rookie astronaut Alan Bean knew what to do. The crew of Apollo 12 were best friends, and their mission enjoyed plenty of laughter. Commander Pete Conrad's first word on the moon was "Whoopee!"

Apollo 13: "Houston, we've had a problem." Those now infamous words were radioed by Commander Jim Lovell after the crew heard a loud, muffled bang followed by a barrage of alarm lights. There had been an explosion. The moon landing was aborted. The big question was whether they could make it home alive.

Apollo 14: The third lunar landing. Alan Shepard, the first American ever in space, returns to walk on the moon. He brings along a golf club head, which he fits to a geology tool handle, and hits an actual golf ball on the moon. It

Apollo 15: The astronauts do three separate EVAs. This is the first time astronauts can truly explore the moon: They have brought along a lunar rover vehicle, an open, dune-buggy-type car enabling them to explore farther from their landing site, as well as on more difficult terrain.

Apollo 16: The astronauts spend three whole days on the moon. Charlie Duke, the CapCom in Mission Control from *Apollo 11* ("*Roger*, Tranquility. *We copy you on the ground. You got a bunch of guys about to turn blue. We're breathing again. Thanks a lot.*") walks on the moon with John Young, looking for signs of volcanic activity. (They don't find any.)

Apollo 17: The first scientist, astronaut-geologist Jack Schmitt, is sent to the moon (all other astronauts have been test pilots). *Apollo 17* is the last of the Apollo missions. Commander Gene Cernan is the last man on the moon: "*We leave as we came, and, God willing, as we shall return, with peace.*"

Index

Glossary

Ablative material: material that absorbs heat and then disintegrates through vaporization

Abort: to cancel prematurely; terminate an action in the early stages

Boilerplate capsule: a full-size craft used for testing, without all the inner details

Contractors: companies that are hired to perform specific work (usually on a large scale)

CSM: (pronounced "C-S-M") command service module; two separate spacecraft joined together

Deploy: to spread out

EVA: (pronounced "E-V-A") extravehicular activity; activity outside the spacecraft — i.e., spacewalk or moonwalk

Fail-operational: with a backup, so if an element fails, the system is still operable

Fail-safe: without a backup, so if there is a failure, there is a short period of time when the system is safe, but it must be abandoned eventually

Friction: a force that resists the motion of two bodies/materials rubbing together

Interface: the place where independent systems meet and communicate with each other

Jettison: to cast off or discard

KC-135: the aircraft used by NASA to train astronauts in zero gravity

Kibosh: something that serves as a check or stop

Landing sequences: a series of procedures followed in a particular order at the time of landing

Launch: to release, catapult, or send off; liftoff

LM: (pronounced "lem") lunar module; originally called the lunar excursion module (the "excursion" part was dropped, but the "e" stuck in the pronunciation)

Loops: headphone walkie-talkie-like communications system enabling members of a group to talk with one another or listen to other groups

Lunar: of, or relating to the moon

NASA: National Aeronautics and Space Administration; the space agency of the United States

Orbit: a path of one body in its revolution (circling) around another

PLSS: (pronounced "pliss") portable life support system, otherwise known as the backpack—the life support outside the spacecraft

Rendezvous: to come together

Simulation: an imitation of the real thing

Terminator: the dividing line between the moon or planet's illuminated and unilluminated disk (the shadow mark)

Translunar: a pathway to the moon